The Spiritual Landscape of Mark

Sr. Grace,
Thank you for journeying
with me through Holy Week,

Bonnie B. Thurston

Blessings,
Bonnie Thurston

LITURGICAL PRESS
Collegeville, Minnesota

www.litpress.org

Cover design by David Manahan, OSB. "Transfiguration," Tretyakov Gallery, Moscow. Attributed to Theophanes the Greek.

1   2   3   4   5   6   7   8

Library of Congress Cataloging-in-Publication Data

Thurston, Bonnie Bowman.
     The spiritual landscape of Mark / Bonnie B. Thurston.
          p.   cm.
     Includes bibliographical references.
     ISBN 978-0-8146-1864-6 (pbk.)
     1. Bible. N.T. Mark—Criticism, interpretation, etc.   2. Bible. N.T. Mark—Geography.   3. Sacred space.   I. Title.

BS2585.52.T48 2008
226.3'06—dc22

                                                                    2008017770

In gratitude for the Sisters of the Society of the Sacred Cross
Tymawr Convent, Lydart, Wales

and for Esther de Waal
who introduced me to Tymawr and to so many who have
immeasurably enriched my life

Contents

Map of Roman Palestine   vi

Introduction   vii

Chapter 1: The Wilderness and the Desert/Chaos and Comfort
Mark 1:1-14; 1:35-39; 6:31, 35   1

Chapter 2: The House and the Sea/Stability and Transition
Mark 2–7   15

Chapter 3: The Valley/Journey and Pilgrimage
Mark 8:22–10:52   26

Chapter 4: The Mountain/Vision and Mystery
Mark 9:2-13 (3:13; 6:46 and 11:1; 13:3)   36

Excursus: Icon of the Transfiguration   44

Chapter 5: The City/Temptation and Corruption
Mark 11–15   49

Chapter 6: The Cross/Suffering, Solitariness, and Solidarity
Mark 14–15   60

Chapter 7: The Garden/Resurrection . . . Perhaps
Mark 14:32-42; 16:1-8   70

Notes   80

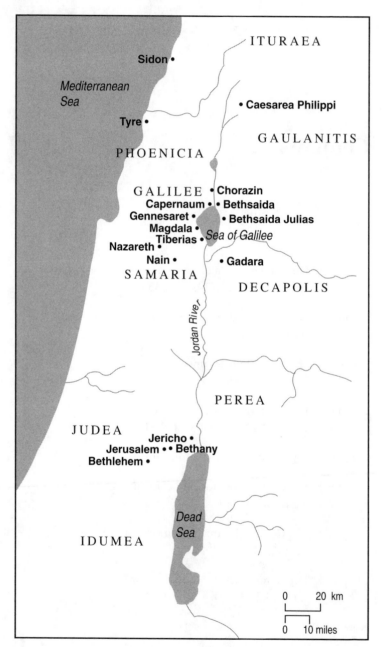

ITURAEA

Sidon •

Mediterranean
Sea

Tyre •

PHOENICIA

GALILEE • Chorazin
Capernaum • • Bethsaida
Gennesaret • • Bethsaida Julias
Magdala • Sea of Galilee
Tiberias •
Nazareth •
Nain •

SAMARIA

• Caesarea Philippi

GAULANITIS

• Gadara

DECAPOLIS

Jordan River

PEREA

JUDEA

Jericho •
Jerusalem • • Bethany
Bethlehem •

Dead
Sea

IDUMEA

0   20 km

0   10 miles

Introduction

Tend only to the birth in you and you will find all goodness and all consolation, all delight, all being, and all truth. . . . What comes to you in this birth brings with it pure being and blessing.
—Meister Eckhart

Genesis

The genesis of this book was a series of retreat talks given to the sisters of the Society of the Sacred Cross at their beautiful, mysterious Tymawr convent. The talks were given in the chapel, and I hope something of its power and serenity might be reflected here for you. Also, I hope the sisters will accept this book as a very small token of my gratitude to them. In "writing up" the talks, I have tried to preserve their oral character, so I take the liberty of speaking in the first person and addressing you directly. I am hopeful that you might make reading the chapters "little retreats." To that end, I have prefaced each with the prayer I used at Tymawr. I think you will find the material most fruitful if you first read the texts of Mark to which I refer. Please don't skip this because you are "familiar with the story." We all think we know the Jesus stories. But sometimes when the guide points out something different, or we look from an unusual perspective, we see something new.

I hope my reading of Mark's text is fresh. I approach the geographical locations in Mark (desert, house, lake, mountain, valley, city, etc.) as symbols (sometimes from a Jungian perspective, but often more generally from the literature of mythology) and then use the symbols as entrances to the text and the life of Jesus. Having written a commentary on Mark, I felt familiar enough with the text and the scholarly discussion around it to experiment with this approach. While you will find scholarship here (I hope!), I have tried very hard not to allow it to weigh down the discussions. For me, looking at the life of Jesus through the symbolic lens of its landscape made St. Mark's gospel dance. It also made startling and challenging connections to my own journey, connections I had not seen before. So before we begin the journey Jesus makes in St. Mark's gospel, a word about the symbolic use of landscape and about the background of St. Mark is in order.

Landscape

When we look at the religious history of the human family, we find that people have "located" holiness in time, space, and persons. In the world's great religions we encounter feasts and seasons of the year, places considered holy, and saints. As C. S. Lewis wrote in *Letters to Malcolm, Chiefly on Prayer*: "It is well to have specifically holy places, and things, and days, for, without these focal points or reminders, the belief that all is holy and 'big with God' will soon dwindle into a mere sentiment."[1] This little book invites you to think about the holiness of space/place/landscape and of its symbolic meaning in the life of Jesus of Nazareth. Please note that already Jesus is designated by the place from which he comes.

From the beginning of human history, there has been a spirituality of landscape. Most fundamentally, God is "up." The Evil One is "down." God, therefore, lives on mountains. Zeus lived on Mount Olympus. Ba'al was the god of the mountains. We may see a reflection of this "in a mirror darkly" in the beloved Psalm 121. El-Shaddai of the Old Testament may be a vestigial memory of Ba'al. Even YHWH's house was built on the Temple Mount, Mount Zion. Likewise, the "Evil One" is "down," so journeys in the underworld are fraught with special danger.

Individually, we, too, are shaped by our geography, the land-scapes of our origins. A "city person" and a "country person" are often superficially quite different. Mountain people are different from plains dwellers or those who live on seacoasts. One reason the sea represents chaos in much biblical writing is that the Hebrews weren't (as the Phoenicians, for example, were) coastal dwellers. I grew up in the "hollers" (narrow valleys between mountains) of West Virginia, and when I first visited the Great Plains, all that sky made me nervous. Where I grew up we didn't see much sky, and often the sun didn't "rise" until midmorning. In the United States, Northerners and Southerners or Easterners and Westerners exhibit different cultural characteristics which I, as an Easterner, learned very quickly when I married a "pioneer" from the West Coast. This is true in the United Kingdom as well. My friends from Cornwall are quite different from my "Geordie" friends. The Scots and the Welsh are related but distinct. My point is that place shapes person.

Place also shapes the prayer life of a person. Writing on July 2, 1948 the American Trappist monk, Thomas Merton, reflecting on the light and landscape around his monastery observed: "I looked at all this in great tranquility, with my soul and spirit quiet. For me landscape seems to be important for contemplation. . . ."[2] Yes. In itself landscape inspires us. But it is also one of the ways God reveals the Divine Self, as even that consummate urbanite, St. Paul, recognized. Writing to those in the city of Rome Paul says: "For what can be known about God is plain . . . because God has shown it. . . . Ever since the creation of the world his eternal power and divine nature, invisible though they are, have been understood and seen through the things he has made" (Rom 1:19-20). Landscape reflects or shows forth its Creator. Landscape is also symbolic or metaphorical, pointing beyond, through itself to other things. And it is that aspect of landscape that was the genesis of this book.

I have a great devotion to Charles de Foucauld, the extraordinary French monk and missionary to North Africa. Something he wrote during the time he lived in Nazareth and worked as a handyman for the Poor Clares' convent there stimulated the idea from which this material arose. Foucauld observed:

> . . . God either calls you to him from Nazareth, as he did with our father St. Joseph . . . or calls you to the desert as he did with your brother Jesus, or calls you to public life, as he has also done for your brother Jesus. . . .
>
> In your heart of hearts don't attach yourself to any of these three ways of life . . . since all three are equally perfect. Be equally ready to take up at the slightest word from God the one among the three which he wishes.[3]

In the passage Foucauld is using "place" or "landscape," in this case Nazareth, the desert, "public life," metaphorically for *types* of life or what we Christians term "callings" or "vocations."

Foucauld's remark led me to think about the "geography" of the life of Jesus. Jesus' life was lived out in a series of real places that have symbolic significance: cave, refugee journey, Jewish village, desert, Gentile villages, lakeside, mountain, on the road down a valley, city, hill, garden. And if one is even slightly aware of the symbolic meaning or Jungian archetypes, such "places" are easily associated with states in the inner life. This is particularly interesting since St. Mark, the writer of the first canonical gospel, uses geography to structure his account and makes his theological points via the narrative he creates. And, of course, then St. Matthew and St. Luke (and to some extent even St. John) follow suit.

Mark

To test this "landscape theory," I thought immediately of St. Mark's gospel both because it is the first gospel and because I spent several years writing a commentary on it and think I am beginning to understand what the amazing writer and theologian Mark was "up to."[4] Almost all commentators think that Mark uses the geographical references in his gospel to indicate the great movements in the ministry of Jesus. The prologue of the story, the ministry of John the Baptist, occurs in the wilderness (1:1-13). The villages, sea, and mountains of Galilee (1:14–6:13) are the scenes of the early and popular ministry of Jesus from which he moves "beyond Galilee" (6:14–8:26) and into strange, foreign territory. The central section of the gospel, in which Jesus teaches those who follow him what discipleship means (8:27–10:52), is narrated as a journey from Caesarea Philippi to Jerusalem, a long trip down the Jordan River valley. And the story climaxes in the city of Jerusalem (11:1–16:8). Within that general framework, Mark writes summary passages to indicate "where we are" in the narrative, and he uses geography symbolically and theologically.

Clearly geography is theological for Mark. Galilee represents an ethnically and racially diverse area in which Jesus' ministry is enthusiastically embraced by the people. Caesarea Philippi, a Gentile/Greco-Roman area is where Peter confesses Jesus as Messiah, thus reinforcing the evangelist's interest in the Gentile mission as he shows Jesus' concern for those "outside Israel." Jesus takes selected disciples "up" a mountain where he is transfigured. Ironically, for Mark, Jerusalem, the place of official religion, the temple, the Holy of Holies, represents opposition to Jesus and religious corruption, *not* the holiest place in Roman Palestine. The more one thinks about Mark's way of telling the Jesus story, the more important the "spiritual landscape" becomes (as I hope this book will demonstrate).

As you read this book, it may help you to know that I hold a very traditional position about the origin of Mark's gospel. Along with the universal witness of the early Church and Greek Fathers, I think Mark was written by an associate of St. Peter in the city of Rome around the time of the Neronian persecution of AD 54–68. This is more or less also the position of Father John Donahue, SJ, an eminent American Markan scholar and author of the Mark commentary in the Sacra Pagina series.[5] Like Paul's letter to the Romans, with which it has many affinities, the Gospel of Mark was written for a "mixed" Christian community of Jews and Gentiles who faced or had recently faced persecution. Mark's gospel is written for those who suffer. In it John the Baptist preached, was delivered up, and was martyred. Likewise, Jesus preached, was delivered up, and was martyred, and raised on the third day by God. Disciples "follow" (the technical term for discipleship in the gospel) their Lord, so can expect to preach, be delivered up, martyred *and* vindicated by God. That was and is a hopeful pattern. It says that after our suffering,

God gives us greater life. Mark's is a gospel, and this is a book, that does not turn away from the fact of suffering.

By literary genre, Mark is a popular work written in *koine* Greek, the *lingua franca* of a large part of the Roman Empire. Its audience was common people, which may be why it seems so "available" to many modern Christians. Some New Testament scholars place it in the technical literary category of "folktale," since nobody official, Jewish, Roman, *or* Apostolic, comes off very well in the narrative. For our purposes that is enough background information about Mark, although reading the chapter on Mark in a good New Testament introduction or a commentary on Mark would enrich your understanding of this gospel. Two commentaries that are particularly helpful for general readers are Morna D. Hooker's *The Gospel According to St. Mark* (1991) and D. E. Nineham's *The Gospel of St. Mark* (1963).

If you glance at the contents of this book, you will see that what I propose to do is to trace Mark's life of Jesus by geography. That is, with the exception of the chapter on the cross, which is somewhat differently focused, I reflect on the location of a particular section of Jesus' life and relate that location to both what it symbolizes and to its function in Mark's view of Jesus and the gospel. To give you a sense of how this works (and so you will know whether to put the book down at this point), I want to begin our journey through the spiritual landscape of Jesus' life with a location that doesn't appear explicitly in Mark's gospel, but that it must assume: the cave.

The Cave

Christmas cards and sentimental carols aside, Jesus was almost certainly born in a cave. If you have had the privilege of visiting the Church of the Nativity in Bethlehem, you very much have the sense of this as you descend the narrow stairs, down below the floor of the nave to the silver star of the traditional place of the birth. Similarly, there is a church built into a cave on the way out of Bethlehem beloved by the local people and known as the "Milk Grotto," the place where, traditionally, Mary nursed Jesus as the Holy Family began its flight to Egypt and joined the long procession of Palestine's refugees.

The locus of the cave is vitally important for us as an archetype of beginnings, of the maternal womb. Caves feature in myths of origin, rebirth, and initiation in many, many cultures. It is an ambiguous image because the cave can both symbolize the nurturing womb and the gloomy pit, the "below place" where monsters, devils, and evil dwell. It symbolizes the unconscious and its unexpected dangers as well as the "Sun Gate" or "Cosmic Eye" from which one emerges from darkness into light.[6] Reflecting on the Paleolithic cave paintings in France, Bede Griffiths in his book *The Golden String* speaks of the cave as a foundational locus of human spirituality:

> . . . from the earliest times of which we have any knowledge, it seems to have been understood that our life in this world is a journey toward God. The journey is from the mouth of the cave, which represents the external world, into the interior which appears as darkness; it is the passage from the outer to the inner world. It is this journey which is represented by the descent of Aeneas into the underworld in search of his father.[7]

Griffiths continues by discussing this pattern in the Odyssey and in the legend of Theseus. "All these stories," he asserts, "are symbols of the same mystery of the search for God which is at the same time the return to our true home. It is represented sometimes as a new birth, a return to the womb, or again as a descent into the tomb by which we rise again to a new life."[8] Paradoxically, the life of Jesus began at the culmination of humanity's spiritual journey. He comes out of the cave, the mystery of darkness, and brings with him light.

To begin in a cave is to begin at the beginning, to begin in the liminal space between earth and underworld. Jesus was born in a cave, and buried in a cave, and from a cave was reborn in resurrection life, the firstborn of many, Paul assures us. To begin in a cave is to begin with the mystery of silence. Certainly Jesus' life began with the great mystery of Mary's "overshadowing" by the Holy Spirit, the great silence of "How can these things be?" To begin in a cave is to begin with the mystery of identity: Jesus' identity as the heavenly One born from the earthly womb and, indeed, the mystery of our own uniqueness as we emerged from our own mother's wombs and have developed and entered into the process of shedding an external identity for an eternal one, a process at the heart of all spiritual journeys. To begin in a cave is to begin with what Evelyn Underhill in *The Spiritual Life* called our "amphibious life:" spirit and body, earth and heaven.[9]

To be of cave origin, to be womb born, is to be compassionate. In Semitic languages the root *rahim*, which is often translated "compassionate," means "womb," the maternal space of nurture from which we move into light. As Bede Griffiths notes, "The 'merciful' is thus conceived as the womb from which all the potentialities in the divine mind are released in creation."[10] We all begin, as Jesus began, in the womb of compassion, God's divine, life-giving compassion. Incarnation must, then, occur in a cave.

It mixes metaphors a bit, but perhaps you can think of reading this book as a sort of cave-in-time, a dark (since you don't know what you will encounter or what will happen), nurturing (since you do know you are perfectly safe with Jesus) "space" from which new life in you might emerge. This is why I have opened this book with the quotation from Meister Eckhart: "Tend only to the birth in you and you will find all goodness and all consolation, all delight, all being, and all truth. . . . What comes to you in this birth brings with it pure being and blessing." We are coming to birth and dying all the time. If we want to grow and flourish, we must devote our energy to what is being born in us and not to what is dying. It is when we cling to the dying that we get into spiritual trouble. To "choose life" is to be open to blessing.

And so we begin our journey through the spiritual landscape of Jesus at the beginning, with a cave, a womb, a birth, new life. The poem "The Kingdom" by R. S. Thomas serves as a wonderful invitation to this pilgrimage and reminds us to set aside our expectations and assumptions (and when we deal with gospel texts most of us have plenty of both) and to come with that most wonderful reality: our neediness. Only the empty cup can be filled. Only the open hands and heart are available to and for God.

The Kingdom

It's a long way off but inside it
There are quite different things going on:
Festivals at which the poor man
Is king and the consumptive is
Healed; mirrors in which the blind look
At themselves and love looks at them
Back; and industry is for mending
The bent bones and the minds fractured
By life. It's a long way off, but to get
There takes no time and admission
Is free, if you will purge yourself
Of desire, and present yourself with
Your need only and the simple offering
Of your faith, green as a leaf.[11]

Chapter One

The Wilderness and the Desert/ Chaos and Comfort[12]

Mark 1:1-14; 1:35-39; 6:31, 35

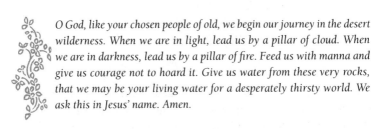

O God, like your chosen people of old, we begin our journey in the desert wilderness. When we are in light, lead us by a pillar of cloud. When we are in darkness, lead us by a pillar of fire. Feed us with manna and give us courage not to hoard it. Give us water from these very rocks, that we may be your living water for a desperately thirsty world. We ask this in Jesus' name. Amen.

"The Desert and the Dry Land"

The desert is a terrifically potent location and metaphor in Scripture. It is a place of terror and tenderness, a place where one is at the mercy of life's extremes and, therefore, completely dependent upon God, who provides what is needed in the desert. As the people of God, our story begins in a garden (Eden), winds its way through various deserts (Sinai, Rift Valley, "beyond the Jordan"), and ends in a city (Jerusalem, the "New Jerusalem"). But it is in the desert that we come to know God and to be constituted as God's people.

The Exodus sojourn of Israel is an exile, but it is also the time when God directly led, fed, and cared for Israel, paradigmatically

1

forgave her sin (after that unfortunate incident with the golden calf), and gifted her with the Law. Christians often get this wrong. Torah is not a burden but God's great gift to Israel. It was in the geographic desert east of the Jordan, and in the desert created by a drought from God, that Elijah was fed by ravens (1 Kgs 17), and it was in the desert where he had fled from Jezebel that an angel brought him food and water and where he met God in what the NRSV calls the "sound of sheer silence" (1 Kgs 19).

For Israel's prophets the desert was a powerful symbol. For Hosea, the desert was a trysting place, a place where the love-pact between God and God's beloved people was to be renewed. According to Hosea, God woos Israel:

> I will now allure her [that is, Israel]
>   and bring her into the wilderness,
>   and speak tenderly to her.
> From there I will give her her vineyards
>   and make the Valley of Achor a door of hope.
>   (Hos 2:14-15)

The idea that God would woo sinful humanity is surprising enough, but this last statement is astonishing because the Valley of Achor (the Hebrew *ay'kor* means "trouble") at the northwest end of the Dead Sea, the desert that formed the northern border of Judah, is where Achan was executed after his disobedience at the time of Joshua (Josh 7:20-26). God is going to make the desert, the place Israel thought of as "trouble," the place of execution, the way to hope! Second Isaiah uses the same striking image when he says that the Valley of Achor will be "a place for herds to lie down" (Isa 65:10).

Indeed, in the book of Isaiah, God's power was manifested in God's ability to transform the desert.[13] Here are a few examples:

> The wilderness and the dry land shall be glad,
>   the desert shall rejoice and blossom;
> like the crocus it shall blossom abundantly,
>   and rejoice with joy and singing. (Isa 35:1-2)

I am about to do a new thing;
>   now it springs forth, do you not perceive it?
I will make a way in the wilderness
>   and rivers in the desert. (Isa 43:19)

For the LORD will comfort Zion;
>   he will comfort all her waste places,
and will make her wilderness like Eden,
>   her desert like the garden of the LORD;
joy and gladness will be found in her,
>   thanksgiving and the voice of song. (Isa 51:3)

In *The Wilderness of God* Andrew Louth has written that the desert, so barren for human purposes, is open to divine purposes.[14] In the desert, where human life is moment by moment at the mercy of the elements, it is God who gives water from the rock and the mysterious, miraculous meal of manna. What I am suggesting by reminding you of these biblical references to the desert is that it is an ambiguous image in Scripture. The desert is the place of danger and abandonment, but it is precisely *in* the desert that God intervenes to save. And this is very good news indeed, particularly if one's immediate future includes a desert, or if one is presently in an arid and empty place.

The Desert Spirituality of St. Mark

No gospel writer understood desert theology better than St. Mark, writer of the first gospel, indeed perhaps "inventor" of this literary form. Mark was probably an urban Christian and certainly had a strong interest in the desert. As noted in the introduction, I think Mark wrote his gospel for Christians in Rome around the time of Nero's persecutions. The traditional dating of the gospel is AD 65–70, making it a gospel written about the dreadful time of the fall of Jerusalem. Mark's original audience may have witnessed the triumphal procession of Titus through Rome in AD 71, when the holy furnishings from the Jerusalem temple were carried through the streets for the rabble's amusement.

One of the reasons Mark wrote was in response to the obliteration of the Mother Church in Jerusalem and the resultant need to preserve the Jesus traditions.[15] Mark wrote in a time of destruction, disintegration, and persecution to a marginal group within a dominant, hostile culture.[16] Mark wrote for a suffering community, a community whose very existence was in jeopardy, a community metaphorically, if not literally, in a desert. Mark has a remarkable number of references to the desert. I found in the gospel at least ten uses of *eremos*, the Greek word for "desert," which is sometimes also translated into English as "wilderness." Where these references occur may surprise you, as they surprised me and gave me new insight into Mark's narrative. First, though, a little etymology.

The word *eremos* is found most frequently in the New Testament as an adjective to describe abandonment or as a noun to refer to a locality without inhabitants, an empty, abandoned, or thinly populated place.[17] This is close to the Latin *desertus*: *de* meaning "from" plus *serere* meaning "to join." A desert is an "unjoined" place. From the root notion of leaving community comes the idea of an uncultivated region without inhabitants, a wilderness. Etymologically a desert is more a wild, uninhabited place than an arid, barren one. The word is not a description of a weather pattern. Although it is "about" something else, R. S. Thomas's poem "The Absence" helps us understand the word.

> It is this great absence
> that is like a presence, that compels
> me to address it without hope
> of a reply. It is a room I enter
>
> from which someone has just
> gone. The vestibule for the arrival
> of one who has not yet come.
> I modernise the anachronism
>
> of my language, but he is no more here
> than before. Genes and molecules
> have no more power to call
> him up than the incense of the Hebrews

at their altars. My equations fail
as my words do. What resource have I
other than the emptiness without him of my whole
being, a vacuum he may not abhor?[18]

The Greek root *erem* means "lonely place" with both connotations of danger to body and soul (in traditional Jewish belief demons were fond of lonely places and ruins) but also of rest, of refuge for the persecuted. As we shall see, both Mark's gospel and the life of Jesus open with these two aspects of the desert in evidence.

Mark 1:1-13

The story line of the gospel begins in the desert with John the Baptist. But even before the narrative begins, Mark introduces a programmatic quotation from the prophets that combines Malachi 3:1 and Isaiah 40:5-6. "See, I am sending my messenger ahead of you . . . the voice of one crying out in the wilderness: 'Prepare the way of the Lord'" (1:2). This is characteristic of the way Mark uses Hebrew Scripture; he combines quotations in such a way that a new assertion is made.[19] Please note that according to this blended quotation it is *in* the wilderness that the Lord's way is prepared. This is true to Isaiah's vision in 40:3: "*In the wilderness* prepare the way of the Lord, make straight *in the desert* a highway for our God" (italics mine). God does not remove the desert, because God has work to be done precisely there. Mark tells the reader at the very beginning that his is a story about a messenger *in* the wilderness, about preparations to be made precisely there. Mark's is a story that unfolds in the context of desert or wilderness.

And so the narrative begins with a messenger in the wilderness, a case in point of the general statement just made. "John the baptizer appeared in the wilderness, proclaiming a baptism of repentance for the forgiveness of sins" (1:4). John appears in the wilderness, the symbol of the time when God was preparing the people for entry into the Promised Land. The wilderness is where people meet God. The Markan John the Baptist material makes the connection between Israel's past and the Jesus story. It is in the desert that God's people find God or, more precisely, are found by God; in the desert they repent; in the desert they find forgiveness; in the desert they rediscover their original inheritance as God's children.

In Mark's narrative people from Jerusalem, the locus of the temple, the dwelling place of God, flock out to the desert to hear John. This gives me pause. What were those people seeking? What was lacking? What did the center of religious life and worship not provide? Why were they choosing the call of the desert over institutional or organized religion? These, it seems to me, are very timely questions.

All the events related in the christological prologue of 1:1-13 occur in the wilderness and are linked by reference to the Holy Spirit. The wilderness may be the abode of demons, but the Spirit of God abides there as well. The desert is the place of repentance and restoration of relationship, but it is also the place of temptation. We read that after Jesus' baptism: "The Spirit immediately drove him out into the wilderness. He was in the wilderness forty days, tempted by Satan; and he was with the wild beasts; and the angels waited on him" (1:12-13). Mark probably expects that some of his readers/hearers will remember the forty years that the Hebrew people were tested in the Sinai desert, Moses' forty days on the mountain, Elijah's trip to Mount Horeb. Interestingly, all these images reappear in chapter 9 in the transfiguration account, which balances the trials of the earthly Jesus with a glimpse of the eternal Christ. We will attend to this material in chapter four of this book.

But something else is going on here. Although Satan is in evidence, the "wild beasts" do not harm Jesus. The curse of Genesis 3 is lifted in the image of harmony between man and beast.[20] The angels wait on (or serve, minister to) Jesus. Here is an image of harmony between human being and heavenly being (in fact, a reversal of the usual roles). The desert may be a time of testing and temptation (more fully treated by St. Matthew and St. Luke), but it is also, on a cosmic scale, potentially a time of restoration of relationship, of receiving the consolations of heaven. The first Sunday of Lent we usually hear the text preached in a way that stresses Jesus sharing temptations with us. Perhaps we also need to hear that the desert time is a time of reunion, of consolation, a time when heaven comes down to comfort earth.

Mark 1:1-13 provides all the information necessary to understand Jesus. It sets forth his titles (v. 1), links him to Israel's story (vv. 2-8), reintroduces his titles (vv. 9-11), and demonstrates their reality (vv. 12-13). Mark opens with the paradox of Jesus' identity: He is the "more powerful" one who is to come, but he is also the one driven into the wilderness and tempted. After a summary of Jesus' preaching in 1:14-16, in 1:16-29 Mark carefully sets out a "typical day" in Jesus' ministry. The Lord calls disciples (vv. 16-20), teaches and preaches (vv. 21-22, 38-39), exorcizes demons (whom he has already met and mastered in the wilderness temptation, vv. 23-26, 32-34), heals (vv. 29-31, 32, 34), and withdraws for prayer (v. 35). This last activity picks up again the "desert" theme.

Mark 1:35-39

After a day of frenetic activity, "while it was still very dark, [Jesus] got up and went out to a deserted place [*eremon topon*, or lonely place], and there he prayed" (1:35). Jesus *chooses* the desert, goes out to a lonely, deserted place to pray. For Jesus, a place without inhabitants is a place where nothing separates him from God; "what He primarily seeks there . . . is the stillness of prayer."[21] John Greenleaf Whittier's nineteenth-century hymn "Dear Lord and Father of Mankind" gets it right: Jesus seeks "the silence of eternity / interpreted by love."

For all the things that matter, Jesus is our example. Here he demonstrates that, as Peter France put it in writing about the Desert Christians of the fourth century, to be silent and alone is to open one's self to influences crowded out of an occupied life.[22] Throughout the Bible, the desert is the place where people meet God, because there is nothing much there to distract them *from* God. Sometimes, as in the life of Jesus, one is driven there (1:12), and sometimes, also as in the life of Jesus, one flees there for refuge (1:35); one chooses desert, seeks it out.

In Mark 1:35-39 the fact that Jesus had to be "hunted" (v. 36) and "found" (v. 37) implies that he had gone to a fairly remote place. Jesus really wanted "desert time," time to seek God in prayer. Christologically, this points to the fact that Jesus' authority and power came from this dependence upon God. But the disciples, those closest to Jesus, don't understand it as, indeed, they misunderstand so much in Mark's narrative. Mark says they "hunted for him" (v. 36). The verbs Mark uses, *katediochen* in verse 36 and *zetousin* in verse 37, are the same he uses for those who later in the narrative seek Jesus to distract him from his true mission (3:32; 8:11) or "hunt for him" or "seek him out" to kill him (11:18; 12:12; 14:1,11, 55).

This image of Jesus choosing the desert, fleeing to a wilderness place, leads me to two kinds of reflection. If the Lord himself needed times of withdrawal, time to be alone to pray, how much more necessary it is for me. Pascal remarked that "all the unhappiness of men arises from one single fact, that they cannot stay quietly in their own chamber."[23] In this context perhaps we might say the *soul* cause of human unhappiness is that we do not know when or how to seek the desert of solitude, silence, and prayer. Jesus went out at night to pray because night is the daily "desert time."[24] We need nights in the desert, nights when, in the words of St. John of the Cross, "*noche que juntaste/Amado con Amada/Amada en el Amado transformada*," nights "when the lover meets the Beloved and is transformed."

Second, I wonder how often I have been like the disciples in this passage. How often have I tried to distract others from the deep need of the human heart for solitude and prayer? Describing Jesus' desert experience in Mark 1:12, Gerhard Kittel noted that it was a period alone with God under the impulsion of the *penuma* (Spirit) "which the tempter tries to disturb."[25] Like Simon Peter did to Jesus, whom have I tried to roust from a *chosen* wilderness in order to get him or her to do something "useful"? For if you go to the desert, you may be sure someone will tell you that you are being useless. Distracting others from their chosen deserts is the devil's work.

After a period of intense activity, Jesus chooses to withdraw for prayer (1:35). After the controversies recorded in 2:15–3:6, "Jesus withdrew with his disciples" (3:7). The word for "withdrew," *anach-*

oreo, is a fascinating one. Its lectionary definition is "to withdraw," "to go away," and also "to return." It is a compound word made up of *ana*, "each" or "each one," and *choreo*, "to make room for." Paradoxically, to withdraw is to make room for; to seek the desert is to prepare to be more fully present. Remarking on Mark 3:7, Mary Ann Tolbert says that although Jesus withdraws after the controversies of 2:15–3:6, the presence of the world continues with Jesus, because he is carrying the world with him in his withdrawal.[26] Mark's gospel depicts Jesus as attempting three periods of private prayer: at the beginning of the Galilean ministry (1:35), in its midst (6:45-46) and at the close of his life when he withdraws to Gethsemane (14:32ff). In each instance, people interrupt him.

When I thought about Mark's gospel in terms of the desert, John the Baptist and the temptation in the wilderness came immediately to mind. I was not surprised to find the word "desert" or "lonely place" appeared in connection with John the Baptist's radical preaching or Jesus' own need for prayer. What I had entirely overlooked was the feeding of the five thousand in chapter 6 and of the four thousand in chapter 8; both occur in the desert. In Mark's gospel, the desert is the place of preparation (1:3), of challenge (1:4), of temptation (1:12), of prayer and rest (1:35), but also of feeding, of being given divine sustenance. Anyone who has read Exodus remembers that the desert is the place where miraculously, but very directly, God feeds God's people. How could I have missed the fact that three times in the story of the feeding of the five thousand in Mark 6:30-44, Mark mentions the desert, the lonely or the deserted place, the wilderness?

Mark 6:30-44

A great deal happens in Mark 6. Jesus is rejected after teaching in the synagogue in "his hometown" (6:1, 3). Jesus sends the Twelve out on mission (6:7-13), and the skillful narrator, Mark, uses that as an opportunity to tell the story of the Baptist's martyrdom (6:14-29). The disciples return from their mission and report to Jesus who immediately (Mark's favorite word) says, "Come away to a *deserted place* [*eremon topon*, italics mine] all by yourselves, and rest a while"

(6:31). And so they "went away in the boat to a deserted place by themselves" (6:32). Thus the feeding of the five thousand opens with two of three uses in the passage of *eremos*, desert, lonely place. It is in the course of trying to get away for rest and prayer that Jesus and the disciples are accosted by "a great crowd," upon whom Jesus has compassion and manifests it by teaching them (6:34). In Mark's gospel, Jesus frequently withdraws *from* the crowd to be *with* the disciples or alone for prayer.[27] But as so often happens with teachers, time gets away from Jesus, and it is the disciples who remind him, "This is a deserted place, and the hour is now very late" (6:35).

Jesus makes it clear that it is the disciples' responsibility to feed the crowd. It is worth noting that Mark uses the word "crowd" thirty-eight times. For him it means the poor, those living at subsistence level, that 90 percent of the population who lived in villages and rural areas and paid two-thirds of their crops in rent.[28] When the five little loaves and two fish they have are put in the hands of Jesus, he "looked up to heaven, and blessed and broke the loaves, and gave them to his disciples to set before the people," and "all ate and were filled" (6:41-42).

Mark relates the story so that we know this is no ordinary picnic. Jesus "ordered them to get all the people to sit down in groups on the green grass" (6:39), the position for dining at a banquet. The great crowd "sat down in groups of hundreds and of fifties" (6:40); the image is that of the order of the Mosaic camp in the Sinai wilderness (Exod 18:21). Jesus' handling of the provisions echoes the essential Eucharistic words and actions earlier recorded by St. Paul in 1 Corinthians 11:23-26. This is a desert feeding designed to recall both God's provision for Israel in the Sinai desert and the Lord Jesus' provision for his people in the wilderness of the world in which they will find themselves. Here, in the desert, is manna, Host, Eucharist. "For Mark, Jesus is a living symbol of plenty, just as the Kingdom of God itself is the advent of the abundant harvest" (4:8, 20).[29]

I tend to think of this as the "miracle of the leftovers" (which are never treated with the respect due miracles in my household!). The community finishes with more than it had in the beginning. But this is also a story about feeding and being fed *in* the desert. In the desert of Sinai Israel had to depend upon God to feed them, because there was no one else to depend upon. Likewise, here in this "deserted place" only God can provide enough. And more than enough. In the feeding of the four thousand in 8:1-10, as well, the setting is the desert. Jesus' disciples (whose memory and intelligence are about equally poor) again ask: "How can one feed these people with bread here in the desert?" (8:4). In both desert feeding stories Jesus is "the embodiment of abundance in the midst of scarcity."[30] It is only the empty-handed who approach God expecting to be filled.[31] Jesus provides abundance *in the desert*. For those on the margins, and those in the wilderness, this is good news indeed!

But notice that Jesus intends to feed the multitude by means of the disciples. "*You* give them something to eat," Jesus says in 6:37 (italics mine). As Elizabeth Struthers Malbon points out in her work on Mark: "The people of the crowd are the chief beneficiaries, the disciples, the chief assistants, of Jesus' ministry of teaching and healing."[32] If what we as his disciples are to provide is not to be the spiritual equivalent of "junk food," then we must deepen our own resources for feeding by precisely the sort of withdrawal, the going away to a deserted place, with which the story opens, which Jesus himself sought. We are not only the ones invited by Jesus to rest in the wilderness; we are those commanded by him to feed others there. Like these first disciples, we may find ourselves "taken, blest, broken and given" to feed (1 Cor 11:23-25; Mark 6:41). Often we are called to meet serious human need at just the point we find ourselves most depleted. Precisely then we become the body of Christ as, in our brokenness, we are blessed and given for others.

Here again in chapter 6 the desert is the place of danger and need as it was for Jesus at his temptation. It is also the locus of rest and prayer as it was for Jesus at the beginning of his ministry, and it becomes the place where people are taught, where they find that Jesus has compassion on them, where the disciples are challenged to action (as John the Baptist challenged his hearers to action in the Jordan wilderness), and where everybody is abundantly fed. The wilderness may be the place of abandonment, but it is also a refuge for the persecuted and a place of salvation, an arid place that, by the mysterious grace of God, blossoms abundantly.

For the L*ORD* will comfort Zion;
        he will comfort all her waste places,
and will make her wilderness like Eden,
        her desert like the garden of the L*ORD*;
joy and gladness will be found in her
        thanksgiving and the voice of song. (Isa 51:3)

Conclusion

The image of the desert is a particularly apt one as we begin our journey through the landscape of Jesus' life. It includes both danger and promise. The desert before us today includes the threat of terrorism and the resultant suspicion of our neighbors, the terrible temptation to demonize difference. It includes a repugnant war in which the mightiest nations on earth bomb others without redress. It includes genocide and widespread starvation and death from preventable diseases. Closer to home, for many it includes the perennial sufferings of disease and depression.

But Mark's desert is an ambiguous metaphor. Like life itself, it embraces the negative and the positive, the terrible and the wonderful. The challenge of desert spirituality in Mark is the challenge to find the first tentative buds that promise blossoms to come, to find the "hope that sends a shining ray" in darkness and aridity, to find God in the desert, to accept the "peace that only [God] can give"[33] *there*—because everywhere else our hands are so full trying to do it all for ourselves. It is a great and terrifying truth that God can only fill the hands of those who approach God empty-handed. Jesus says "Blessed are the poor" for a reason, and it isn't economic.

Writing of the desert, Alessandro Pronzato explains:

> The desert is the threshold to the meeting ground of God and [humans]. It is the scene of the exodus. You do not settle there, you pass through. One then ventures on to these tracks because one is driven by the Spirit towards the Promised Land. But it is only promised to those who are able to chew sand for forty years without doubting their invitation to the feast in the end.[34]

In the Bible, the first lesson of the desert is the relinquishment of human control and dependence upon God alone, relinquishment of human concern so that God alone can be the focus of our attention.[35] When God comes clearly into focus on the horizon of life, a very curious thing happens; we discover that the face of God is imprinted on the faces of the neediest of those among us. The moment in which the mouth full of sand becomes the mouth full of manna is the moment when my neighbor's hunger becomes as important as my own.

Mark's picture of Jesus feeding the multitudes in the desert is certainly the fulfillment of Isaiah's prophecy that the desert shall blossom. But Jesus feeds by means of the disgruntled disciples. Mark's disciples, as indeed we, ourselves, have some things to learn about need. It is my suspicion that we are driven by the Spirit into the wilderness precisely to learn about need, to find that, in many ways and on many levels, we, too, are needy. We must learn this lesson in what W. B. Yeats called "the deep heart's core" because it is only through the open door of the solidarity of human need that the power of God can enter the world to feed, to make the desert blossom. We can never open that door through our own ingenuity.

So the desert is the place of promise for the one brave enough to go there, to remain there long enough to learn the bitter and liberating lesson of her or his own need. In the introduction to his collection for Lent entitled *The Desert* John Moses writes:

> The desert is a place of truth. The experiences of the desert expose our weaknesses, search us out, test us. The desert can . . . be the place of discovery. . . . the meeting ground of God with all who learn to rest in faith alone. The promise remains that the desert shall rejoice and blossom, that waters shall break forth in the wilderness, that the burning sand shall become a pool, and the thirsty ground springs of water. [The desert] speaks of the hidden life, of endurance, of testing, of simplicity, of self-abandonment, of the silent prayer of the spirit. It bears witness to the absolute priority of God.[36]

We could appropriately close on this high note of theological rectitude. But ending with a story is more in the desert tradition. Accounts of the Desert Christians of the fourth century report that people went out into the desert to seek the men and women who had made eating sand their regular diet. They asked them for a word, a bit of manna to sustain their own journeys. And I have one for you. It comes from that wise "children's book" by Antoine de Saint-Exupéry, *The Little Prince*. You probably remember the story. The airman has an accident and comes down in the Sahara Desert, where he meets what he first describes as "an odd little voice," whom we come to know as the little prince. In chapter 24, eight days after his crash in the desert, the airman has drunk his last drop of water. He and the little prince trudge along for several hours in search of water. They find none. Night falls. A conversation about the beauty of the desert ensues. It closes: "What makes the desert beautiful," said the little prince, "is that somewhere it hides a well. . . ."[37]

This is my word for you: What makes the desert beautiful is that somewhere it hides a well. May you find it, drink deeply, and bring others to share the gift of its living water. For this is the desert pattern of Jesus' own life, and, as Mark teaches us, disciples are to do as their master does.

Chapter Two

The House and the Sea/
Stability and Transition
Mark 2–7

 *Lord our hearts, our bodies, our minds are, indeed, restless until they find rest in you. May we so completely know you as the home of all our longing that, when the storms of life blow at our little boats, we may rest secure in your eternal love for us, shown in Christ Jesus, our Lord, in whose name we pray. Amen.*

The Geography of Roman Palestine

Although I, myself, loved it as a child, I am told that geography is not a favorite subject. But for understanding the life of Jesus, it is crucial to know the contours of Roman Palestine. You might want to look at the map on page vi in connection with the opening of this chapter. There you will see that the hill country of Galilee fans out from the Sea of Galilee (also called the Lake of Gennesaret). Traveling south from the lake, the Jordan River runs down the Rift Valley through Judea and below Mount Zion and Jerusalem to the west, and into the Dead or Salt Sea. It is "dead" because it has no physical outlet, a fact worth pondering in itself. That which takes in but doesn't "give back," dies.

Mark uses this geography in two ways. First, Mark's narrative traces the life of Jesus according to the "route" we have just mapped out. Second, for Mark geographical places are theologically and symbolically important. Galilee, an ethnically mixed and relatively poor area, is the locus of popular support for Jesus and home to most of his early disciples. Jerusalem, on the other hand, while it is a more concentratedly Jewish area and relatively better off economically, represents for Mark opposition to Jesus and the place of the passion. The scribes and Pharisees come from Jerusalem to spy on Jesus, to report back, to plot against him.

The way Mark uses geography gives us leeway to "play" with locations, to see what we can learn and tease out by thinking theologically and symbolically about them. The early days of Jesus' ministry and the early chapters of Mark's gospel are set in Galilee, and within that geographical designation there are two important loci, the house and the lake.

"House" and "Home"

"House" is a neutral word for most of us, a structure that provides shelter. "Home" is a word that usually has strong emotional resonances, which is why advertising uses it so extensively. But sometimes those resonances are positive and sometimes negative. If we came from stable, happy homes, the word conjures up feelings of safety, nurture, comfort, joy, and love. If we came from unhealthy families, "home" might have been a place of terror or danger or at least unpredictability. As I thought about this, I came to the conclusion that for most of us "home" is the place that, emotionally, we either run to or run away from. Home is the place from which we launch. Home is also the place we are seeking. We are, according to the writer of Hebrews, "seeking a *home*land" (Heb 11:14, italics mine).

Where was your home? Was it a place you wanted to leave or a place to which you long to return? Where is home now? Where will home be? These are all fruitful questions for prayer and reflection. And they are relevant to our understanding of Jesus who began his life as a refugee and who, according to Luke at least, as an adult had "nowhere to lay his head" (Luke 9:58).

Symbolically, houses are also images of the universe. Ancient houses had smoke holes in the roof and water drains in the floor and were literally an axis joining heaven, earth, and the underworld. Arab or Damascene houses enclosed a garden, an image of paradise. And in the center of the garden was a fountain, living water at the core. No wonder medieval monastic architecture patterned itself on the Damascene model. The square houses of modernity are oriented to the cardinal points of the compass. Interestingly, the house is a feminine symbol, at least intentionally the sanctuary, the maternal protection of the womb.[38] There is a deep, psychological reason for the "attachment" of woman to home, although in the current climate of "political correctness" one hesitates to point it out.

Home is also the ordinary place of day-to-day life. It is where we work or from whence we go to work. It is where we learn and grow and develop . . . or don't. Galilee is "home" in this sense to Jesus. Nazareth, where he grew up, was his "hometown" where, presumably, he had a very normal childhood with his mother and St. Joseph, from whom he must have learned carpentry, as Mark 6:3 calls Jesus "the carpenter." Certainly the *Abba* language (which only Mark records, the other evangelists use the Greek *pater*[39]) of Jesus' prayer is profoundly connected to house/home as well as to the *pater familias* organization of the Roman Empire. When I teach the "Father God" passages in the New Testament, I suggest to students that the invitation to call God "Father" isn't primarily about gender but about the intimacy of the family, the healthy domestic sphere. It is linked to the "inheritance" language so prevalent in St. Paul. To be invited to call God "Abba" is an extraordinary invitation into God's family circle, an image of profound intimacy and ease. (Parenthetically, I think that Rom 8:12-17 reinforces the point I am making here.)

"Home" is also the place of the secret life of Jesus, of those years about which we know absolutely nothing. It is the christological manifestation of the fact that nobody knows what goes on in a home or in a family but the people who live there. Charles de Foucauld was absolutely taken by the idea of the "hidden life of Nazareth" and used it as an image of the sort of life, hidden in Christ, to which we are all deeply called. He understands that, as God did with our Lord, God calls some of us from a secret life of Nazareth to a life of public proclamation. But all of us remain in the hiddenness of Nazareth. Our life, like Paul's, is literally "hidden with Christ in God" (Col 3:3). Foucauld made the following observation on May 18, 1905: "The life of Nazareth can be followed anywhere; follow it in the place where it is most helpful to your neighbors."[40] On July 22, 1905, he wrote: "Jesus has set you up forever in the life of Nazareth. Missionary and solitary lives are only the exception for you as for him: carry them out every time his will indicates it clearly; as soon as it is no longer indicated, return to the life of Nazareth."[41]

Ideally at least, in our world "home" is where we go to be ourselves. It is where our masks come off, where we expand psychically and spiritually, where we are ourselves. "Home" is where we do not have to get ourselves up in psychic fancy dress. This is why heaven is our ultimate home. It is the place of our complete belonging, where we are fully known, where we will be our perfected selves. The "Abba" concept of Jesus and St. Paul is taken up by St. John when he calls us "children of God." "Beloved, we are God's children now; what we will be has not yet been revealed. What we do know is this: when he is revealed, we will be like him, for we will see him as he is" (1 John 3:2). Heaven-home is the source of our ultimate nurture and identity.

Unlike St. Matthew and St. Luke, St. Mark suggests that Jesus may have had a house in Capernaum, the headquarters town of the Galilean ministry (2:1, 15; 3:19). Mark is certainly very interested in Jesus' life "in the house." Jesus withdraws into the house to try to get away from the busyness of his public life (7:24). Jesus does definitive miracles in the house (see, for example, 1:29-31 and 5:35-43). In the house, Jesus explains in detail to his disciples the public teaching to the crowds outside. Jesus and Mark both use the image of the house in their teaching. Let me simply enumerate a few examples:

First, Jesus withdraws into the house to get away, often without success. In one manuscript tradition, Mark seems to suggest Jesus had a house at Capernaum; verse 2:15 says that "he sat at table in [his] house."

- "The whole city was gathered around the door" (1:33).

- After a preaching and healing trip around Galilee ". . . he was at home. So many gathered around that there was no longer room for them, not even in front of the door" (2:1-2).

- After being on the mountain and calling and sending out the Twelve, "He went home" (3:19b).

- "He set out and went away to the region of Tyre. He entered a house and did not want anyone to know he was there. Yet he could not escape notice" (7:24). The Syrophoenician woman seeks him *inside* the house. (What sort of woman does *that*!?)

Second, Jesus does important miracles in the house.

- In Simon and Andrew's house he heals Simon's mother-in-law, who, by arising to serve (*diekonei*), becomes one of the first disciples/deacons (1:29).

- People gather outside the door of house where Jesus is, clamoring for healing (1:33). (And see also 6:53-56.)

- It is in Jairus' house, with the three inner-circle disciples, that Jesus shows the extent of his power, and Mark prefigures the resurrection, by raising the dead little girl to life (5:21-24, 35-43).

- Jesus does the long-distance miracle for the Syrophoenician woman from the house (7:24-30).

Interestingly, in light of the fact that the house is a feminine symbol, all these "in-house" miracles are for females, girls, or women.

Third, Jesus gives advanced teaching to his disciples in the house.

- "When he had left the crowd and entered the house, his disciples asked him about the parable . . ." (7:17). We link this to 4:10: "When he was alone, those who were around him along with the twelve asked him about the parables." We must imagine this as a mixed group of men and women. Mark 15:40-41 must be read back onto the whole gospel: the women at the crucifixion who "used to follow him and provided for him when he was in Galilee; and there were many other women who had come up with him to Jerusalem."

- "He explained everything in private to his own disciples" (4:34). The disciples get private exposition from Jesus because he knows of the work they will have to do later after he is gone. Again, these "disciples" included men and women. Jesus and the disciples are in Capernaum and "when he was in the house he asked them, 'What were you arguing about on the way?'" (9:33).

- "And in the house the disciples asked him again about this matter [divorce]" (10:10).

I connect this special "in the house" teaching with our word "ecumenical," which, of course, has as its root *oikos*, the house, the family. It interests me that the really big miracles, the christologically revelatory ones, and the advanced teachings occur in private, in the house, within the family circle so to speak. The private, nurturing "in house" context allows important things to occur. I am reminded that some of the teachings of Christianity are to be reserved for those "in the family" and would be quite nonsensical to outsiders.

Fourth, Jesus and Mark use the image of the house in their teaching:

- "If a house is divided against itself, that house will not be able to stand" (3:25).

- "No one can enter a strong man's house and plunder his property without first tying up the strong man" (3:27).

- "Prophets are not without honor, except in their hometown, and among their own kin, and in their own house" (6:4).

This last saying of Jesus reminds us that for Mark, too, house and home are ambiguous images. House/Home can be a strongly exclusionary image. Let me give just two examples. First, in verse 3:19, Jesus is at home, and his family, who have decided he is certifiable, come to get him, and they find scribes from Jerusalem there who also think Jesus is possessed. Mark says "his mother and his brothers" were "standing outside." They are not, at this point, part of the in group to whom Jesus gives special teaching. Mary and his brothers send a message in to Jesus, who uses the occasion to redefine family as those who do the will of God together. For Jesus, "family" is not necessarily the biological family. Related to this point, we might ask, "Whom are we excluding at home?" It is a fair and frightening question.

Second, in the extremely moving story in 5:1-20 of the Gerasene demoniac, recall that the story begins in the cemetery with the demoniac living among the tombs. He is excluded from home and hearth, permanently living rough. Jesus subdues his demons (and disposes of a lot of the local livestock in the process!). Not surprisingly, the man begs to be allowed to go with Jesus, who says, "Go home to your friends, and tell them how much the Lord has done for you, and what mercy he has shown you" (5:19). Jesus sends him back to the very people who had excluded him from home, back to the very people who remembered him as a maniac! It may be the most difficult assignment in Mark's gospel.

For Mark, "house" is the inner place, the place into which we try to withdraw from the work that we are called to do in the world. As this "inner place," the house was where Jesus gave special, more advanced teaching to his disciples and where he did the miracles that made it clear who he was. But home is also an ambiguous symbol where, when we are doing exactly the thing God calls us to do, we may not be recognized, or we may be thought crazy and sent by God to the very people who do not recognize the most important things that have ever happened to us.

It seems to be psychologically the case that unless we have some sense of home, or a stable place to which we belong, we are unable to make much progress in life, to travel very far. You can't travel unless you have a home from which to go and to which to return.

That is why I have treated the image of the house before that of the lake/sea. "House"—for good or ill—is the stable place. "Sea/Lake" is the place of transition.

The Lake/The Sea

If "home" is the deep, inside place in the early ministry of Jesus, the "lake" is the outside, public venue. "Sea" (*thalassa*) is the Greek word Mark uses, although, actually, "lake" probably calls up a more appropriate image in our minds. In ancient mythologies, lakes symbolize the Earth's eye through which inhabitants of the Underworld gaze up at us. Artificial lakes were built by temples to symbolize the abiding powers of creation. Seas, because of their vastness, were images of the primal, undifferentiated formlessness, "the Abyss" in Old Testament terms (more on this in a moment). Everything comes from the sea and everything returns to it. It is an image of transformation and rebirth and the transitory condition of life.[42]

There are so many references to "sea" in the opening chapters of Mark because it was, of course, a major geographical feature of Galilee and the source of much of its economic prosperity both through fishing and tax collection on goods that were transported around and on the sea. In terms of the narrative of Mark's gospel, the Sea of Galilee is the public locus of Jesus' teaching and functions like a train service; it gets Jesus and the disciples from place to place. They cross back and forth because that was easier and faster than walking around the shores. Jesus frequently teaches crowds beside the sea (2:13; 3:7; 4:1; 5:21; 6:54). And, naturally, where the crowds gather there are healings. "Sea" is synonymous with the public life and ministry of Jesus, with the active work of teaching and healing.

Mark also uses a sea journey as a transitional device in the narrative, as this list of examples makes clear: "Let us go across to the other side" (4:35); "They came to the other side of the sea" (5:1); "When Jesus had crossed again in the boat to the other side" (5:21); "And they went away in the boat to a deserted place by themselves" (6:32); "Immediately he made his disciples get into the boat and go on ahead to the other side" (6:45); "When they had crossed over" (6:53).

What this suggests is that the sea is also an image of transition, of moving from place to place. We will speak more of this when we speak of the valley, but I am much moved by the idea that Jesus and the disciples had many transitions to undergo. His life repeated what anthropologists of religion call the "monomythic pattern": leaving, liminality, return. Transitional times are not easy times; they are times when everything is up for grabs, when we can be psychically and spiritually a little seasick! And yet they are "on the way times," times when we are moving to a new place, and new places are always, in part, places of promise. The presence of a lake or sea in the life of Jesus is a reminder that life is, like the sea, constantly in flux.

There are two great "sea stories" early in Mark, the stilling of the storm (4:35-41), and Jesus walking on the water (6:45-52). To conclude this chapter, let's look very briefly at the first of those two. All the stories from 4:35 to 6:6 are, in some sense, stories about fear. In Mark's gospel the opposite of faith is not unbelief but fear.[43] The stilling of the storm in 4:35-41 is part of a block of miracle stories that runs through 5:43, in which Mark demonstrates the extent of Jesus' power. In doing these miracles Jesus shows his authority over the natural world (stilling of storm 4:35-41), the spirit world (Gerasene demoniac 5:1-20), the physical body (woman with flow of blood), and life and death (Jairus' daughter 5:21-43). I suggest that in 4:35-42, the main character in this story (after our Lord) is not the cowering disciples but the sea.

The ancient Hebrews were shepherds and city dwellers, not sailors/explorers like the Phoenicians. For them the sea is an image of chaos. In the Hebrew Scripture YHWH controls the sea and subdues the chaos monster Tehom ("the Deep"). The storm on the sea is a metaphor for evil forces in Psalm 69:1-2 and 14-15:

> Save me, O God.
>   For the waters have come up to my neck.
> I sink in deep mire,
>   where there is no foothold;
>
>   . . .
>
>   rescue me from sinking in the mire;

> let me be delivered . . . from the deep waters.
> Do not let the flood sweep over me,
>   or the deep swallow me up.

Similarly in Psalm 89:8-9 the ability to control the sea is a divine power: "O Lord God of hosts, / who is as mighty as you, O Lord? . . . You rule the raging of the sea; / when its waves rise, you still them."

And in Psalm 46:1-3, the faithful know that God saves in the storm:

> God is our refuge and strength,
>   a very present help in trouble.
> Therefore we will not fear, though the earth should change,
>   though the mountain shakes in the heart of the sea;
> though its waters roar and foam,
>   though the mountains tremble with its tumult.

One final example comes from Isaiah 43:2a: "When you pass through the waters, I will be with you; / and through the rivers, they shall not overwhelm you."

Jesus asleep in the back of the boat with his head on a pillow while the storm rages is a picture of complete trust in God's sustaining and protective care (compare Prov 3:24b "When you lie down, your sleep will be sweet"). In contrast, the disciples literally "feared a great fear" (in the NRSV, "were filled with great awe") (4:41). When in verse 39 Jesus stills the storm with a formula of adjuration for a storm demon (Greek: *pe-thi-mo-so*), he is assuming an authority that the Old Testament gives to God alone. Here is a picture of Jesus versus the forces of chaos personified by the sea. Mark makes it very clear who is in control, and the big question is the one with which the miracle closes: "Who is this . . . ?" Mark's answer is clear from the narrative. This is characteristic of Mark's method: what he wants us to know, he shows us in the narrative. Not for Mark the discourses of Matthew or the parables of Luke. For Mark theology is found in the narrative itself. We know who Jesus is by what Jesus does.

Jesus enters the most severe experience of human beings, chaos in a time of transition (according to our reading of the image of the sea), and brings order out of it, indeed, the text says he effects "a dead calm." The pattern is threefold: (1) the great chaos of the sea, (2) the great fear of the disciples, (3) the great calm brought by Jesus. To put the matter theologically, the place of transition is often the theophanic place, the place where God is most clearly manifested to us. The place of chaos can be the point of theophany. It is *in* the period of liminality and transition, in the stormy sea crossings of life, when we may be most fearful and frantic, that Jesus reveals himself most clearly as who he IS. And that, it seems to me, is very good news.

Chapter Three

The Valley/Journey and Pilgrimage
Mark 8:22–10:52

 *Lord Jesus, when you invite us to follow you, you invite us to be a pilgrim people, a company on the move, on a journey. Teach us to travel lightly through this world and to encourage our fellow travelers. Whether we journey inward or outward or wander, stay with us, and when evening comes lead us home, for we ask in your own, dear name. Amen.*

Introduction

In the last chapter we considered the images of house and lake in the geography of Jesus. The first was an image of home, of stability, nurture, the everyday, the secret life in Christ that for all of us who love and follow him is what is really going on no matter what else is going on. We also noted that "home" can be an exclusionary image. The second image, the lake or sea, is an image of change, and change can be frightening. For good or ill, the Christian life is not a call to settle down. Ironically, we are both rooted people and travelers or pilgrims. The image of change leads to the image of pilgrimage. We are called to be a people on the move, a people who travel light in this world and through this world.

Here is what I have in mind: Jesus is always offering us invitations, and usually, in reality or metaphorically, they involve leaving where we are and going somewhere else. "Come and see." "Follow me." "Go and make disciples." You get the idea. The challenge of the *oikoumena*, the household of Jesus, is to be a "home on the move," a stable place in transition. This is not too surprising. The root story of Jesus' own people is the story of the Exodus: leaving, traveling, entering a new space. As we have noted, this is what anthropologists of religion call the "monomythic pattern." In most religious traditions there is a mythology of leaving the familiar and experiencing a journey, a liminal time when the old is left behind but one has not arrived at the new place. The third part of the pattern is arrival at a new place and as a new person because of the experiences of the journey. In the great literature of the West this pattern is often encountered. The *Iliad, Odyssey, Decameron* of Boccacio, and Dante's *Divine Comedy* all follow this pattern, and even our own English language *Canterbury Tales* is a riff on this theme.

Mark places his journey motif right at the center of his gospel. Most Markan scholars think the central parts of the gospel are 8:22–10:52, the discipleship section, and 11:1–16:8, the passion narrative. Mark frequently and accurately is called a passion narrative with an extended introduction. In this middle bit of Mark, 8:22–10:52, what we see is a familiar sight in the Greco-Roman world: a peripatetic teacher and his students, a sort of traveling seminar. Jesus uses the journey from Galilee to Jerusalem as an opportunity to do two crucial things: first, to tell the disciples, very explicitly, what will happen in Jerusalem; second, to try to teach them the meaning of discipleship, what it means "to follow." *Akoloutheo*, follow, is a technical term for discipleship in Mark, not just the ordering principle in a procession.

You might want to consult again the map on page vi. It is something between sixty and seventy miles from Tiberias on the Sea of Galilee to Jericho, the city from which one quite literally "goes up" to Jerusalem. Straight south from Tiberias, one passes through the Jordan Valley or the Rift Valley, one of the lowest places on earth, well below sea level, and through wilderness that ends, none too cheerfully, in the Dead or Salt Sea. The other way to go from Galilee to Jerusalem, the route that St. John's gospel reflects, is through Samaria with the attendant religious and political problems that entails. Either way, the journey is difficult. From Jericho to Jerusalem is a journey of roughly fifteen to twenty miles, uphill all the way and through some of the most barren territory I have ever seen. No wonder Jesus sets the parable of the Good Samaritan on the Jericho Road!

My point is that the difficulty of the geographical journey is an exterior template of the journey the disciples are asked to make internally and spiritually. They must come to understand a very hard lesson, that Jesus is to be crucified. They must learn that Jesus is the *kenotic* or self-emptying hero described in Philippians 2:6-11. Discipleship requires of them the same dismantling of ego, of the world's sense of what identity is. Over and over again they must come face to face with themselves as they are, and then change. In my experience this is never a particularly pleasant experience. A journey through a valley is a journey through a "low place." Sometimes in the life of discipleship we are called to travel through low places.

The valley is a potent symbol in religious mythology. Valleys are the spiritual ways and means of passage. Valleys are empty and, as such, they are open to receive celestial influences. They are hollow channels through which waters can run, sometimes suddenly causing terrible floods like those that occur in the wadis of Palestine. Valleys are the symbolic complements of mountains (which we shall consider in the next chapter). Valleys are the places for fecundating change "where Earth and the waters of Heaven come together to provide rich harvests and where the human soul and God's grace unite to produce mystic revelation and ecstasy." "All valley symbolism concentrates upon this fecundating marriage of opposing forces in the synthesis of opposites at the heart of the integrated personality."[44]

God's road runs through valleys. Isaiah says that every valley shall eventually be exalted (Isa 40:3-6). "Eventually" is the operative word. Mark's Jesus story begins with John the Baptist in the Jordan River Valley and with his association with Isaiah's promises. "Shall be" is future tense. The valleys are not yet lifted up, but the valley time, the low time, plays an important part in the eventual exaltation, as indeed it does here in Mark's story of Jesus.

Richard of St. Victor remarked that the ark of the covenant was revealed to Moses first upon a mountaintop and then in a valley, "where extraordinary revelation given on the peak became a familiar part of normality."[45] And this is the great temptation, isn't it? To let what we learn on the heights of revelation be lost when we come "home" to the valleys of everyday living. It is why I think Jesus' charge to the Gerasene demoniac is so difficult (5:19). I suspect it is also why St. Matthew's gospel closes with risen Jesus promising to be with the disciples in "Galilee," the ordinary, day-to-day locus of their lives (Matt 28:10).

Mark 8:22–10:52

Let us begin our pilgrimage down the Jordan Valley by noting how carefully Mark structures the central, middle section of his gospel as a journey, first by making reference to actual places and second by shaping the narrative in parallel structures.

First, Mark makes references to geographical places, thus giving the reader a sense of following along the journey geographically. If you trace these places on the map, you will find a very confused route. Clearly, they are not following the "mapquest" directions. Here are examples of Mark's geographical references:

- "They came to Bethsaida" (8:22), a town at the northeast side of the Sea of Galilee.

- "Jesus went on with his disciples to the villages of Caesarea Philippi; and *on the way* he asked his disciples . . ." (8:27). The geographic turn is an odd one if the destination is Jerusalem. Here is a reminder that Mark's geography is symbolic more than literal. The villages of Caesarea Philippi are some thirty miles northeast of the sea. They are Greco-Roman villages and comprise a mixed racial area, the locus of Peter's great confession. Mark wants Jesus in this Gentile area for purposes related to his own, original community.

- "They went on from there and passed through Galilee. He did not want anyone to know it; for he was teaching his disciples"

(9:30-31a). Now, at least Jesus and the disciples seem to be headed south. Jesus is known as a healer/teacher in Galilee. But he doesn't want this to be a public trip. He has private things to teach the disciples, like the teachings we saw in chapter 2 "in the house."

- "Then they came to Capernaum; and when he was in the house he asked them . . ." (9:33).

- "He left that place and went to the region of Judea and beyond the Jordan . . ." (10:1). Again, the geography is odd. The company has turned west toward the Mediterranean.

- "As he was setting out on a journey . . ." (10:17).

- "They were on the road, going up to Jerusalem, and Jesus was walking ahead of them; they were amazed, and those who followed were afraid" (10:32). This is a very important text. Jesus takes the lead. Theologically, if we are disciples we follow. In the narrative some of the disciples must have understood the lessons being taught privately on the journey and in the house. Are they now afraid of what they are going to face in Jerusalem? Are they afraid of the journey itself? Why are they afraid? In Mark the opposite of faith is not unbelief but fear, as we learned in the account of the stilling of the storm. This is a great Markan motif; one can believe or one can fear. Those are the two choices. Again, Mark has his own, persecuted community in mind as he tells Jesus' story. Fear must have been rife among them. And, unfortunately, fear is a primary motivating factor for most people whether or not they realize it. Thomas Merton says fear is the root of war.[46]

- "They came to Jericho. As he and his disciples and a large crowd were leaving Jericho . . ." (10:46). An oasis city and the site of one of Herod's palaces, Jericho was the gateway to Jerusalem and all that would happen there.

Clearly, Mark wants the reader or hearer of the narrative to envision a journey. On this journey, disciples follow Jesus who is teaching them what it means to follow and how to follow. The point is that we learn discipleship on the way. This central section is clearly indicated or framed by two stories of blind men, 8:22-26 and 10:46-52. In the first Jesus must make a couple of attempts to cure the blindness, a way of telling us that less-than-perfect sight/understanding is not good enough. In the second, the blind man takes the initiative to come to Jesus and is immediately healed. This pairing of like stories is a literary device called an "inclusion"; two similar stories "frame" a block of material. When we remember that sight is a metaphor for understanding, we understand that this narrative unit is supposed to reveal something to us, but what?

Within the frame of the blind men brought to sight, Mark inserts three passion predictions by Jesus that allow him to instruct his followers on the nature of discipleship. Everything in the section is related to the meaning of "Christ/Messiah" or to discipleship. Within the framework, each of the passion predictions is similarly structured to call attention to their importance. That is, 8:27-38, Peter's confession, provides a pattern that Mark repeats twice more.

Geographic Reference:

8:27 "to the villages of Caesarea Philippi,"
9:30 "through Galilee," and
10:1 "the region of Judea and beyond the Jordan."

Passion Prediction:

8:31 "He *began* to teach them . . ." suggests there is more to
   come;
9:31 repeats the prediction, more detailed and explicitly; until
10:33-34 gives the passion narrative in outline. Is Mark suggesting that Jesus, himself, gains greater insight into what
   is coming as the journey progresses?

Disciples' Misunderstanding:

in verse 8:32 when Peter rebukes him,
at verse 9:34 when they ask who is greatest,

and in 10:35 when two of them request the seats of honor in
the kingdom.

Further Teaching:

8:34–9:1;
9:35ff; and
10:42ff.

   In this journey section Mark's Jesus is teaching the disciples
about his impending passion and about what it means to *be* disciples.
Implicitly Mark, writing for a persecuted community, is linking the
suffering of Christians with the suffering of John the Baptist (who
prepared the way) and with Jesus (who is the Way). Disciples follow
Jesus. If Jesus suffers, disciples will suffer. In his book *Disciples and
Discipleship*, Ernst Best wrote, "What does it then mean to follow
Jesus? It means to drop in behind him, to be ready to go to the cross
as he did, to write oneself off in terms of any kind of importance,
privilege or right, and to spend one's time only in the service of the
needs of others."[47] Discipleship is about dismantling the false self,
the ego with its focus on self. Discipleship means putting my life at
the service of someone else's.

   This is a sort of psychological Rift Valley, isn't it, to renounce
completely any assertion of self? But we are not going to stay in the
valley. We are headed for Jerusalem and to Calvary and eventually
to resurrection . . . but the Rift Valley and the *Via Dolorosa* first. As
African American Christians sing, "If you can't bear the cross, then
you can't wear the crown." In any case, the way Mark tells the story
makes the resistance of the first disciples understandable.

   This central section of Mark's gospel addresses two problems
that may well reflect the circumstances in Mark's own church: first,
the likelihood of persecution and martyrdom, and second, the desire
for status and domination. Somehow they have a familiar ring, don't
they? Many Christians in our world do literally face martyrdom
for the faith. But we will, too, socially and psychically, if we seek
to serve and follow and be disciples as Jesus teaches rather than as
we choose.

One of the root problems in human interaction, in community living, is status and domination. We want to be accorded the respect due to our perceived (by us, of course!) status as professor, priest, religious sister, parent, boss, teacher, supervisor—whatever. We feel shamed if we "don't get no respect," as the American comedian Rodney Dangerfield put it. The human family hasn't progressed much beyond the shame and honor culture of the first century. Domination is about power. If I don't feel very good about myself, one way I can feel better is to lord it over (bad turn of phrase!) somebody else. Little people have to assert dominion over others. Big people can serve others. So much of the misery of our world has its roots in status and domination, which is also the root of much misery in our personal lives. All this is clear in Mark 8–10 as Jesus tries to teach his followers another way.

The Metaphor of Journey/Pilgrimage

To conclude, let's go back and look again at the metaphor of journey/pilgrimage. In Mark's narrative, Jesus has initiated a journey as a way of getting the disciples out of their habitual situations, the day-to-day routine that can dull the spiritual senses and keep one from "seeing." Jesus was a consummate psychologist; he knew that a change of scenery—geographically, intellectually, and spiritually—can be a very good thing. The framing stories of the blind men healed tell us that this section of the gospel is going to be about new understanding. The lessons Jesus wants to teach are learned "on the journey." Discipleship is learned "on the way." And, of course, early Christianity was known for a long time as "The Way." All of this exactly fits the great journey and pilgrimage motifs in human culture.

In literature, journeys are often metaphors for the quest for or discovery of self or of a spiritual center. The traveler is really a pilgrim, one who, dissatisfied with his or her circumstances, has undertaken a journey in search of another ideal. Often the pilgrimage is in search of a master or spiritual teacher. In Mark, however, the teacher initiates the journey, and this reflects what we know of God in the Christian spiritual life. God is always the initiator, always reaching out to us, even when we are hiding in the bushes or eating pig slop in a foreign land.

Journeys or pilgrimages "give expression to a deep-seated desire for internal change and a need for a fresh range of experience. . . ."[48] Odysseus, Hercules, Menelaus, Sinbad, the Wife of Bath, and Pilgrim in *Pilgrim's Progress* are people who are searching. The remarkable thing about the pilgrimage motif in Mark is that here the Master, the Teacher, is not hidden, not the one who must be sought through trials; rather he is the one who not only initiates the journey but also says, "I'll go with you. I'll lead you there. Follow me. I'll go first and face the Final Enemy so that you will know how to face it yourself." This is extraordinary and extraordinarily wonderful.

Diana Eck, professor of the history of religion at Harvard University, says there are

> three basic types of pilgrimages. First, outward-bound journeys go "to the frontier in a kind of metaphorical sense." Second, homeward-bound journeys are "somehow back to where we started, where our major stories are acted out." These are journeys of return. Finally in wandering or peripatetic pilgrimage, "the point is not so much one's destination at all, but the journey itself, the discipline of being on the road."[49]

It is worth thinking about what type of pilgrimage we are on at this stage of our life's journey. Am I returning to something or seeking something new? Even thinking in terms of "outward bound," "homeward bound," or "wandering" is intriguing to me. The other possibility, I suppose, that Eck hasn't introduced is "lost." I hesitate to use it because if we are on the road with Jesus, if we are following the way of discipleship, if we are following the way of the cross, we can't in any ultimate sense be lost, although we may feel lost. I am reminded of a story about the American frontiersman Daniel Boone, with whom my father's Welsh family went west through the Cumberland Gap. Someone asked Boone if he were ever lost. He replied, "No, but once I was bewildered for three days." Apparently, days of "bewilderment" are part and parcel of pilgrimage even for great explorers.

The phrase "the discipline of being on the road" also speaks very deeply to me as I think about this middle section of Mark's gospel. Discipline and discipleship have the same root. "Disciple" in Greek is *mathetes*: disciple, pupil, follower, in Mark, one who learns *by* following. In Latin "disciple" is a compound: *dis*, apart, and *capere*, "to hold." Discipleship is holding apart (from societal expectation? the "usual" way of doing and being?), or it is being taken apart in order to be put together in a new way. Training is what makes disciples. Discipleship is discipline. And we learn this "on the road" so to speak. Life is our—um—disciplinarian!

Last winter I read a wonderful book by Phil Cousineau, *The Art of Pilgrimage*. It began with this statement: "My travels were moving question marks."[50] This is my image of the disciples in Mark 8–10. They are traveling question marks. And I wonder if we are not, in some sense, all traveling question marks. We are the living, breathing mystery of incarnation and identity. We are full of questions about the meaning of our lives and discipleship. And the place where we will get the answers is precisely *on* the journey.

Cousineau says that "inside every question is a quest trying to get out."[51] It is very fruitful to ask ourselves what our questions are. Thomas Merton, the American Trappist monk, once remarked that we are better known by our questions than by our answers. What are the deepest questions of your heart right now? And what is the quest, the journey, the pilgrimage that they might initiate?

I close this leg of our journey with Jesus by quoting a Hasidic saying: "Carefully observe the way your heart draws you and then choose that way with all your strength."[52] Variations of this saying occur frequently in spiritual teaching. If the heart has been prepared and purged by the pilgrimage of discipleship, it is a trustworthy guide for the next stage of the journey. What is the desire of your heart? Are you following its leading? And if not, why not?

Chapter Four

The Mountain/Vision and Mystery
Mark 9:2-13 (3:13; 6:46 and 11:1; 13:3)

Lord Jesus, we want to be those chosen to go with you to the holy mountain. Protect us from our desire to see more than what we can assimilate. Transfigure us, Lord. Remake us in your image, but at a pace we can endure, we ask in your name. Amen.

Introduction

Ordinary life and spiritual life are the same life. Thomas Merton wrote in *Thoughts in Solitude*, "If you want to have a spiritual life you must unify your life. A life is either all spiritual or not spiritual at all."[53] We have the daily, domestic life of the house and the life of the journey. Sometimes the journey has the shining character of pilgrimage, but a lot of the time it manifests the trudging, putting-one-foot-in-front-of-the-other-to-get-on-with-it aspect. Happily, life also has what we call "mountaintop" experiences, experiences of illumination and piercing joy. And while they are illuminating, they are also often mysterious.

The geography of Jesus exhibits exactly this pattern. Jesus and the disciples go from carpentry, fishing, and farming, business as usual in Galilee, to a journey of learning. And in the midst of that

journey there is a mountaintop experience we call the "transfiguration of Jesus." As is always the case in Christian spiritual life, the
initiative for this amazing experience is Jesus, and the real activity is
done by God. Jesus takes Peter, James, and John away with him to a
mountain. Already the first hearers of the story would be interested:
first, because if I am correct about the gospel's provenance they know
or knew of Peter, and second, because mountains were places of
theophany, of God's manifestation (more on this in a moment). On
a mountain, God transfigures Jesus for the disciples' sake.

This theophany in Mark 9:2-13 is one of the most difficult passages in the gospels to understand and interpret, and I probably ought
to have my head examined for including it, but if we are "doing" the
geography of Jesus, how can we exclude it? [54] Some years ago I was
discussing this text with adult Master of Arts in Theology students.
Someone in the class said: "The Bible is a lot like a child passing on
a parent's message. They do the best they can without understanding
the whole thing. Some things get scrambled along the way, but one
gets the gist." Indeed. But what *is* the gist of this passage? Some
students of Mark's gospel think it is an immediate fulfillment of 9:1
or a divine attestation of Peter's confession in 8:29. Others suggest it
is a misplaced resurrection appearance and really belongs at another
place in the narrative, perhaps after the enigmatic 16:8.

This latter doesn't seem to me helpful, especially in light of the
fact that it is characteristic of Mark the writer to organize the narrative to make theological points. Mark's overall "meaning" is discovered in the organization and context of any given story. So I am
taken with the suggestion of C. S. Mann that the transfiguration is
a theologizing of the passion predictions; it shows us how suffering
is glory.[55] And I would add that it demonstrates this to precisely
the inner circle of disciples, Peter, James, and John, before whom
Jesus demonstrated the extent of his power when he raised Jairus'
daughter (5:21-43), and who will become the leaders of the early
community of Christians after his own death. They will need this
glimpse through the veil.

Remember that the transfiguration occurs at nearly the spatial
center of 8:22–10:52, the journey of passion and discipleship framed

by the healing-of-blind-men stories. Perhaps the transfiguration is Jesus' attempt to heal aspects of the blindness of Peter, James, and John. Jesus is revealed to them with Elijah (who represents the prophets) and Moses (who represents the law), and the heavenly voice says, "This is my Son, the Beloved; listen to *him!*" (9:7, italics mine). The narrative closes with a discussion of Elijah, who was popularly understood as a harbinger of the Messiah. In Mark's narrative, Elijah was understood to have come in the person of John the Baptist, and he was treated by Herodias much as Jezebel treated Elijah! Elijah and John both suffered for their religious vision. Jesus' transfiguration is set in this context, so that the fate of John the Baptist seals his own fate.

The Canon of the Feast of the Transfiguration in the Orthodox Liturgy gets it just right: "How mighty and fearful is the vision that was seen today! The visible sun shone from heaven, but from the earth there shone upon Mount Tabor the spiritual Sun of Righteousness, past all compare." Let us now turn to an examination of how Mark treats this amazing event in Jesus' spiritual landscape.

Mark 9:2-13

Everybody knows that religions build temples on mountains because God is "up." The Acropolis of Athens is an example. So is acro-Corinth where the temples were placed. There is the symbol of Mount Kaf in Islamic lore, the "post" or "pillar" Allah created to support the world. And all we monotheists share Mount Zion. God lives on holy mountains. The rest of us mortals carry on our lives in the lowlands. So when the narrative "goes up," we have come to expect a theophany.

Because geography for Mark is symbolic, he isn't very careful to designate the literal places on a map. Both Mount Tabor in Galilee and Mount Hermon much farther north, northeast of the Sea of Galilee toward Damascus, are traditional sites for the transfiguration. I think the better claim is for Tabor in Galilee from which one looks out on beautiful, fertile land, northwest to Nazareth, northeast to Tiberias and the Sea of Galilee, south toward Nain and the Rift Valley. But the point is the mountain, not which mountain. Exodus 24:9-10 are paradigmatic verses for our understanding of mountains. "Moses and Aaron, Nadab, and Abihu, and seventy of the elders of Israel *went up, and they saw the God of Israel*" (italics mine). God is "up." Mountains are the traditional location of God's appearances in the Hebrew tradition. Moses meets God on Mount Sinai and is given the law in Exodus 19–20. Elijah meets God in prayer on Mount Carmel (1 Kgs 18) and on Mount Horeb (1 Kgs 19:11-18). The call of Isaiah is a vision in the temple which is on Mount Zion in Jerusalem. One meets God on mountains; they are the symbol of transcendence.

Mountains rise up from earth toward the heavens. They are liminal places between the earthly and the heavenly. In most cultures, therefore, they are "holy places." To ascend mountains is to go closer to God. Both Saints John of the Cross and Teresa of Avila use the image of ascent to describe the spiritual life. So did John Climacus, John of the Ladder, centuries earlier. But the prophets had said so long before. Isaiah 2:2 and Micah 4:1 record:

> In days to come
>   the mountain of the Lord's house
> shall be established as the highest of the mountains,
>   and shall be raised above the hills;
> all the nations shall stream to it.

Mountains are theophanic in the life of Jesus, the places where we glimpse something of his "otherness." Think of the Sermon on the Mount, the transfiguration, the Mount of Olives, Calvary's "Mountain," the Mount of Ascension. When we see Jesus on a mountain, we are very likely to be seeing him in something approaching his glory, his role as Lord. Mountains are likely to be places of what systematic theologians call "high christology."

But let me not wander too far from Mark's text. What is it that *happens* in 9:2-13? Whatever takes place is communicated right at the beginning by the term "was transfigured" in verse 2, *metemorpsothe/metemorothe*. Students of Greek will note that the word is a passive. Whatever happened on the mountain was done *to* Jesus. He was recipient of the action. You are probably familiar with what scholars call "Divine Passives." Jews didn't use God's Name. Instead, in writing they used the passive voice with the understanding that God was the actor. Paul uses this grammatical construction extensively in his letters. It is also used here and, interestingly, every time reference is made to Jesus' resurrection, it is in passive voice.

Metemorphothe is a late Greek technical term for a change of form or for some effulgence from within, so it echoes for us the meaning of *exousia*, authority, as Mark uses it in chapter 1. There was something from within Jesus, out of his being, that made people pay attention to him. The term has strong roots in Jewish apocalyptic thought. Here it seems to suggest that Jesus is the recipient of an exchange of human form for glorious form or divine form. Jesus goes to the mountain, and God changes him in some essential way. The root of the verb is a noun, *morphe*, a Greek philosophical term used by Aristotle to express true Being, a never-changing reality. One's *morphe* is his or her essential nature, Being, "the real person." This is how the term is used in the Christ hymn that Paul quotes in Philippians 2:6-11 when he says, "Jesus, who . . . was in very nature [*morphe*] God" (my translation).

As I was thinking about changes, I remembered a passage in 2 Corinthians which I find mysterious, wonderful, and promising. In chapter 3 Paul is writing to the Corinthians, explaining that the competence of ministers "is from God" (3:5). He goes on to use the image of Moses who had to put a veil over his face when he came down from Mount Sinai. Then comes the passage that is so remarkable: "Where the Spirit of the Lord is, there is freedom. And all of us, with unveiled faces, seeing the glory of the Lord as though reflected in a mirror, are being transformed into the same image from one degree of glory to another" (3:17-18).

Paul is suggesting that, like Peter, James, and John, we are "seeing the glory of the Lord," not face to face but reflected as in a mirror. And, like Jesus, we are "being transformed"—it's the same word, *metemorphothe*—"into the *same* image" (italics mine). Paul uses the same word for humans that Mark uses to describe Jesus' change. Paul seems to be suggesting that we become what we see on the mountain. For me this is a breathtaking idea. You and I can receive transfiguration, be transfigured as Jesus was to reflect Divine Glory. Paul suggests a profound connection between seeing or gazing on Jesus and being transformed into his likeness. This goes even beyond what John says in his first epistle: "Beloved, we are God's children now; what we will be has not yet been revealed. What we do know is this: when he is revealed, we will be like him, for we will see him as he is" (3:2). Paul seems to be saying it has been revealed. We can see it and become what we see. Indeed, *morphe* suggests it is what we are *supposed* to be, our true or essential nature. Would it be too radical to say that we are to become the place where people see God?

The Orthodox Church has a term for this transfiguration of the Christian person: deification in Christ. The goal of Christian maturity is to become a "little Christ." The transformation is done "to" us as we turn wholeheartedly, openly, fully toward the Christ. As Thomas Merton says, "You are made in the image of what you desire."[56] We sing in the old hymn, "We would see Jesus," and our desire to see him forms us in his image. It is a very fruitful thing to ponder what it would mean to be transformed and transfigured. What would it mean to me—and to those around me who "see" me—for me to be transfigured? Or even to desire transfiguration so thoroughly that I began volitionally to seek it? This may be the key question posed by the image of the mountain. What is the mountain to which I must go for transfiguration? Mountain climbing is difficult and dangerous work, but the views from the summits are amazing.

Two other aspects of Mark's account in 9:2-13 require attention. The first is another odd little linguistic bit which I noticed as I was perusing a Greek dictionary. Two words in Greek are exactly the same save for the breath mark. *Horos* (hard breath mark at the outset) means "mountain, hill, mount." *Oros* (soft breath mark at the beginning) means "limit, boundary." I very much wonder whether somewhere in the dark back room of history some ancient Greek understood that a mountain was also a boundary. Mountains do function this way in human history. Nations mark boundaries along mountain ranges. Think, for example, of the Pyrenees or the Alps. Cities are protected by being built on hills. The mountain thrusts upward toward the heavens, but also marks a boundary beyond which the human cannot go. But, of course, people want to "go beyond," so mountain climbers are still killed on places like Zermatt and in the Himalayas. This is a very vivid image of *hubris*, pride, overreaching God's set limits for us. In Exodus 19, the Hebrews are told not to touch the mountain. It is a boundary the ordinary human must not transgress. (Thank goodness for extraordinary humans!) Mountains are transformative places and thus places of considerable danger. Transfiguration isn't "safe."

Second, there is this business in verses 5-6 of Peter wanting to make "booths." Throughout the gospel, Mark singles out Peter for special attention. Personally, I think this is in part because Mark the evangelist is recording the reminiscences of Peter. From the time of Papias, it was the universal witness of the ancient church that Mark wrote down what Peter said in Rome. There are several things we might say about Peter's response to Jesus' transfiguration. (Some scholars think his own recollected response is recorded in 2 Pet 1:16-19.) The first is Mark's own explanation in verse 6. Peter just blurted out what came to mind because he was dead frightened. Alas that Peter, James, and John missed the meaning of the cloud that overshadowed them (v. 7). The cloud is the symbol of God's presence to guide and protect. It recalls the leading cloud of the Exodus and the Shekinah over the ark in the Jerusalem temple.

"Booths" is also suggestive. Remember in chapter 8 Peter rebuked Jesus for speaking of his, that is, Jesus' passion? Most commentators think this is because for Peter "Messiah" was a term with political and military overtones. The "Messiah" would liberate Israel from the Romans as David had done from the Philistines or Judas the Maccabee from the Greeks. "Booths" are built at the Feast of Tabernacles, a nationalistic feast. Does Peter want Jesus to lead the nation to political freedom as Moses did? To put down Israel's enemies as Elijah did? Does Peter think of Jesus in the line of Israel's military deliverers, Joshua, David, Judas the Maccabee?

Or is it simpler than that? Does Peter simply want to prolong an episode that verse 8 makes perfectly clear was intended to be temporal, indeed ephemeral? Poof! Moses and Elijah are gone. In the very next verse, "they were coming down the mountain." Maybe Peter didn't *want* to come down the mountain. Maybe he *did* understand that to come down the mountain, to continue the journey to Jerusalem, was to return to the suffering and servanthood of discipleship. Or maybe he knew it just meant more walking, more putting one foot in front of the other, more of the "same old, same old."

Peter's response is very characteristic of our responses to "mountaintop experiences." We manage to get ourselves organized to go away on a retreat. And sometimes on retreat we do, indeed, see Jesus face-to-face. We have great spiritual consolations and extraordinary experiences in prayer. And we don't want them to end. We want to build "booths." But it doesn't work this way. Like Peter, like the Gerasene demoniac, Jesus sends us back home to minister there, in the very place where it will be most difficult to speak of what the Lord has done for us. This is particularly acute in families and parishes and religious communities where we are jolly slow to allow that those we know and live with might have been transfigured!

In the spiritual landscape of Jesus in Mark's gospel, the journey has to continue. The Mount of Transfiguration is an important experience. It calls at least three of the disciples from the ordinary and ho-hum to a new vision, to seeing Jesus transfigured, to facing the possibility of being transformed. But then the journey has to continue. There is more work to do, more lessons to learn, a long way to travel to Jerusalem. For Peter, James, John, even Jesus, the journey was not finished. It did not end on the mountain of transfiguration. And it does not end for us, either. We must finish the journey, travel up Mount Zion, enter the city of Jerusalem and face all that transpires there.

Excursus

Icon of the Transfiguration

Sometimes we break a journey for a little rest. Sometimes in the course of an academic book there is an "excursus," a break in the process of the argument to give further information or an expanded perspective on a point. This excursus is a brief respite in this book and on our journey with Jesus. It is another way of looking at the landscape of a Markan story. It give us a chance to "come away and rest" before we finish the very difficult journey to city, cross, and garden.

There is a sense in which Mark's gospel rests on the pillars of three theophanies or manifestations of God in Jesus: the baptism, the transfiguration, the cross/resurrection. The central pillar, the transfiguration, is both a historical event and a prophetic vision given to the inner circle of Jesus' disciples. Another way to approach it is through its representation in an icon. To prepare to "read" the icon, let us recall another account of the transfiguration, one perhaps recorded in retrospect by St. Peter:

> For we did not follow cleverly devised myths when we made known to you the power and coming of our Lord Jesus Christ, but we had been eyewitnesses of his majesty. For he received honor and glory from God the Father when that voice was conveyed to him by the Majestic Glory, saying, "This is my Son, my Beloved, with whom I am well pleased." We ourselves heard this voice come from heaven, while we were with him on the holy mountain. (2 Pet 1:16-18)

Orthodox Christians believe that icons make present the events/ figures they depict. So in examining this icon, the one reproduced on the cover of this book, we are placing ourselves, like Peter, James, and John, *at* the event and *in* the story. In the Eastern Orthodox Church, the Feast of the Transfiguration is the last great feast of the liturgical year. It occurs forty days before the Feast of the Holy Cross with which it is profoundly linked theologically (and which we shall mention in the chapter on the cross). The canon of matins for the feast includes this beautiful verse:

> O Master of Heaven,
> and King of the earth,
> you have the power over hell, O Christ!
> The apostles beside you represented the earth,
> Elijah the Tishbite came from heaven,
> and Moses from the dead
> in order to sing to you in one voice . . .

The icon of the transfiguration reproduced on the cover follows the traditional pattern developed in the tenth or eleventh century and the Russian Novgorod School of the "writing" of icons. In some ways it is the least "representational" of icons because the event it manifests is so mysterious. In it, the eye is drawn first to Christ at the center, hovering over the mountain, not standing on it. This tells us immediately that what is before us is a manifestation of christology and, in particular, the opening up of a moment of eternity in time. How does one describe eternity in the temporal realm? Three aspects of the icon suggest its meaning: the geographical setting, the geometric figures, and the human/divine persons in the icon.

Geographical Setting

When there are mountains in icons we know that what is before us is a theophany of some sort, a manifestation of divinity. Here on three mountains, we see (from left to right) Elijah, Jesus, Moses, each on his own mountain because each is associated in the Bible with a different mountain experience. The mountains themselves are depicted as wildernesses (there is no vegetation on them), as, indeed, were the mountaintop experiences of the characters.

Geometric Design/Arrangement

The mountains serve to divide the icon in half horizontally. At the top of the mountains are the heavenly figures, at the bottom, the earthly figures. Heavenly figures are vertical. Earthly figures are horizontal or bowed down or kneeling, indicating the proper response of the earthly to the heavenly.

The two determining geometric shapes in the icon are the circle of light around Jesus, and the rays emanating from his figure. The circle around Jesus is light, and it is cut by rays of light coming from his person. Traditionally, God is often represented in icons by a black circle or half circle at the top of the icon. The circle represents infinity and perfection, the blackness, mystery. We know some things about God, but very few know God directly, thus the inscrutability of the black circle. Here, one glimpses the suggestion of the dark circle behind Jesus. He seems to be emerging *from* it, the light of the World from the mystery of God. Light and dark are the mysteries of God, here visually set before us in the person of Jesus.

The three grayish rays pointing downward from the figure of Christ are a way of telling us that the action here depicted is Trinitarian. The triangles behind Jesus symbolize the Trinity. This is reinforced by the fact that, geometrically, things occur in threes in the icon. There are three mountains, three men at the top, three men at the bottom, three rays linking the heavenly and earthly.

Divine/Human Figures

The icon follows closely the Synoptic Gospel narratives of the event. At the top are Elijah (representing the prophets), Jesus (the Son of God), and Moses (holding a tablet of the Law and representing Torah). Elijah and Moses flank Jesus, and each gestures toward him, indicating they have understood the message of the Voice that said, "Listen to him." Jesus fulfills both prophecy and Torah. Elijah and Moses are rich parallel figures and serve as theological foils to

Jesus. Both had visions of God (Moses in Exod 33 on Mount Sinai, Elijah in 1 Kgs 19 on Mount Carmel). Both had mysterious endings. That is, neither of them dies in an "ordinary" way. Elijah was taken to heaven, and we aren't sure what happened to Moses. So both foreshadow the unusual ending of Jesus which is yet to come.

At the bottom are (left to right), Peter, John, and James. Matthew and Mark say that the apostles fell to the ground when they saw this vision. Their different physical positions represent the different ways that people receive divine revelation. Peter, with his graying beard and hair, is represented as older. He reaches up toward Jesus, as we know from the gospel, offering to build booths. John has curly hair and is beardless. He is the youth in the icon. His hand cups his chin in "thinker" pose. James is bearded and older and seems to be reaching up to shade his eyes from the light. The drapery around John and James suggests motion, that they have just fallen. The image of the three men reminds us that some turn toward Jesus and some turn away. Even *within* the community of disciples and, indeed, the inner circle of Jesus' friends, the mysterious differences of response to Jesus are in evidence.

At the center of the icon and of its message is the transfigured Jesus, the vision of the triumphant Christ. He is dressed in white and gold, Imperial colors, as an attempt to represent the light that the gospel accounts describe. He hovers over the mountain as something more than a human figure, and he offers those who view the icon the traditional gesture of blessing. (The circle formed by his three fingers represents the Trinity, and his two vertical fingers, his divine and human natures.) Holding the scroll which only he can open, he hovers between the "quick" (the living at the bottom of the page) and the "dead" (the historical figures at the top) as Lord of both.

Summary/Conclusion

In the transfiguration, human beings saw "uncreated light." John of Damascus described the transfiguration as "a temporal glory of the Son of God." It manifests the timelessness of Christ's glory. The Eastern Church venerates the transfiguration as a communication of the incommunicable. The Eastern Church distinguishes between God's essence and energies. In essence, God is absolutely transcendent. God reveals the Divine Self to us through energies in the form of grace and divine light. St. Gregory Palamas said the experience of divine energies often takes the form of light, the light perceived by Peter, John, and James at the transfiguration and seen by saints such as Simeon the New Theologian and Seraphim of Sarov.

> The Fathers of the Eastern Church (Gregory Palamas in particular) used the term *uncreated energies* for the grace (the gift of God). God reveals himself to us, gives himself to us in his infinite love, through the divine energies which radiate from the three persons of the Trinity. Christ's body . . . appears on Tabor penetrated by the rays of divine light. He is the reflection of the beauty of the Father. He makes the uncreated light, the gift of the Spirit, to shine on the world.[57]

So for Orthodoxy the transfiguration is one of the most complete symbols of God's manifestation, communicating to us what we can never, in this life, fully "see" or know. Like Peter, James, and John, we are given this glimpse to strengthen us for the journey that continues.

Chapter Five

The City/Temptation and Corruption
Mark 11–15

 *Our hearts can be fortified cities with the gates closed and barred against you, Lord. We are not brave enough to ask you to batter our hearts. Give us courage to know our interior castles as they are, not as we would like them to be, not as we would show their facades to others. As you pitched your tent among us, come again and dwell within us and lighten our dark corners. Amen.*

Introduction

The truth is that what goes up has to come down. It is, so far as we know at the moment, a law of physics. But it is also true of the spiritual life. After the high moments of revelation, our theophanies, our mountaintop experiences, which like Peter we want to build little huts to prolong and preserve, we "come down." Coming down the mountain is a symbol for returning to the ordinary, the day-to-day, the ho-hum, the "same old, same old." And sometimes it is even worse. After a great upswing and series of insights in the spiritual life, we "crash and burn." Pride (especially spiritual pride) goeth before a fall. At least that's how it often works for us.

The truth of this observation, that "downs follow ups," is shown to us by Mark in the life of Jesus. In chapter one, after the baptism when the heavens open, the Spirit descends, and the heavenly voice comes to Jesus (1:9-11), the very next verse of the narrative says that same Spirit "drove him out into the wilderness" (1:12). After the "up" of the baptismal theophany comes the "down" of the temptation in the wilderness (1:12-13). If this is so for Jesus, why would we expect our life pattern to be otherwise?

Having this pattern in mind helps us to interpret the irony of the symbol of the city of Jerusalem in the Gospel of Mark. Whereas in biblical tradition generally people go "up" to Jerusalem, and this is a geographic necessity since the city is built on a hill, Mount Zion (remember, for example, the Psalms of Ascent, 120–134), for Jesus going to Jerusalem is "going down": down the Jordan Valley, down from Galilee and the scenes of his popularity, down to betrayal and ultimately, in God's most astonishing irony, "up" to coronation on the cross. So let us begin this chapter not with the archetypal symbolism of the city, which we shall consider later, but with the city of Jerusalem and how it functions in Mark's gospel.

The City of Jerusalem and the Temple in Mark's Gospel[58]

The recognition of Jesus by blind Bartimaeus in Jericho at the end of chapter 10 is the narrative's preparation for Jesus' entry into Jerusalem in chapter 11. Chapters 1–8 occur in and around Galilee. In chapters 9–10 Jesus and the disciples are constantly "on the move," reminding us that discipleship is learned "on the way." Chapters 11–16 occur in and around Jerusalem, particularly in the temple precincts. This is a great Markan irony. For most Jews in first-century Palestine, going to Jerusalem meant going to meet God, going to the "holy city" that held the beautiful and newly-refurbished Herodian temple which so impresses Jesus' disciples at the outset of chapter 13. They thought of the temple as the locus of God's presence with God's people. But, for Jesus, going to Jerusalem is going to the place of religious corruption, personal opposition, rejection, and death. Jerusalem has been a negative symbol throughout the Gospel of Mark. Let me give you a few examples.

After the title of the book in Mark 1:1 (which gives the reader information no one in the story has and so makes the whole narrative a bit ironic), we are introduced to John the Baptist via a blended quotation from Malachi and Isaiah. John, as we noted earlier, is a "desert" person. Mark records: "And people from the whole Judean countryside and all the people of Jerusalem were going out to him, and were baptized by him in the river Jordan, confessing their sins" (1:5). Why does Mark write: "*all the people of Jerusalem were going out to him*"? What was it that was lacking in the holiest city in Judaism that led people *away* from the city and into the wilderness/desert? Let me ask the question more sharply: What was missing in official, institutional religion that people had to leave the locus of its operation and go out into the desert and confess their sins? It seems to me that Mark, albeit obliquely, is saying something very dark about Jerusalem (and perhaps about institutionalized religion).

And then we begin to see Jerusalem in the context of opposition to the preaching and ministry of Jesus. In chapter 2 scribes question Jesus' activity in Capernaum (2:6); scribes of the Pharisees are unhappy with Jesus' dinner companions (2:16). In chapter 3 Pharisees and Herodians, people who were actually political enemies, plot together against Jesus (3:6). Mark states explicitly that scribes "came down from Jerusalem" and said that Jesus "has Beelzebul, and by the ruler of the demons he casts out demons" (3:22). Chapter 7 begins with Pharisees and scribes who came from Jerusalem, apparently to interrogate Jesus and his disciples. I could multiply the examples, but you see what I am getting at. Scribes and Pharisees and Herodians have Jerusalem as their headquarters. If we read the narrative from Jesus' point of view, Jerusalem is from the outset a source of, at best, tension and, at worst, open opposition. Jerusalem represents "the enemy."

As previously discussed, in the journey narrative in chapters 8–10 Jesus begins, "quite openly" as Mark says (8:32), to speak of what will happen *in Jerusalem*. Each of the three passion predictions in that section becomes more explicit than the last until, at

10:33-34 Jesus says: "See, we are *going up to Jerusalem*, and the Son of Man will be handed over to the chief priests and the scribes, and they will condemn him to death; then they will hand him over to the Gentiles; they will mock him, and spit upon him, and flog him, and kill him; and after three days he will rise again" (italics mine). These two verses, in fact, outline precisely the passion narrative in chapters 11–16.

In Mark's gospel Jerusalem symbolizes opposition to the ministry of Jesus. Is it too harsh to say that, symbolically, Mark suggests that religious officialdom is in conflict with the kingdom of God? Jerusalem is the place not of life but of death. And this is a supreme Markan irony because what is of God is always, *always* life giving, tending toward greater life. Mark 11–16 *does* evince an ascending motif, but it is not "going up to Jerusalem," but going up to the cross, an idea that St. John's gospel uses extensively (and which we shall consider in the next chapter). The movement is into Jerusalem and toward the temple, the symbolic center of Jewish life. But the temple is the Markan symbol of Jesus' conflict with the Jewish leadership groups, a conflict that dominates chapters 11–12.

The following is my understanding of the structure of Mark 11 and 12:

> **Entry into Jerusalem** (11:1-11): This event is ambiguous and probably not the "triumphal entry" of my Palm Sunday childhood when we marched around with palm branches singing songs of victory (and whacking each other with the palms if we could get away with it!).
>
> **The Fig Tree Inclusion** (11:12-26): We have met the structural device of inclusion in the chapter on the journey. Here two parts of a narrative about Jesus' encounter with a fig tree (vv. 12-14 and vv. 20-25) frame the story of the temple cleansing (vv. 15-19). Rather than an indication of the petulance of Jesus, the cursing of a fig tree functions as a prophetic sign-act indicating what will happen to the temple and a symbolic teaching that "prayer" will replace "place" in Christian spirituality.[59]

Encounters in the Temple (11:27–12:44): A series of stories in which Jesus "bests" every group in Judaism in debate. In a shame-and-honor culture such behavior will not win him friends. This unit parallels earlier controversy sections (for example, 2:1–3:6). In terms of genre, a "controversy narrative" is one in which someone asks Jesus a question not to learn or for inquiry but specifically to trap or test Jesus. The encounters with Jesus proceed as follows:

(11:27–12:13): The chief priests, scribes, and elders, in short the Sanhedrin question Jesus about authority;

(12:13-17): The Pharisees and Herodians (normally enemies) ask Jesus about taxes, a hot-button issue geared to show a person's ultimate loyalties: Judaism? Caesar? (God?)

(12:18-27): The Sadducees (who do not believe in resurrection) ask Jesus a question about marriage in resurrection life.

(12:28-37): Opposition of official Judaism to Jesus has been progressive in Mark, moving from questioning to plotting to condemning to death. This section, too, works by accretion. Jesus has silenced all the major leadership groups. Just as my point was not that Jerusalem and the temple were objectively bad or evil places, Mark doesn't think Jews in general are evil. Indeed, many of the Christians in Rome for whom he wrote the gospel must have been Jews (as is also reflected in Paul's letter to Rome). So Mark includes an encounter that is not a controversy story but a scholastic dialogue in which a scribe asks a real question. The key to being a "goodie" or a "baddie" in Mark is not whether or not one is a Jewish leader but how one responds to Jesus, as the positive figures of Jarius and Joseph of Arimathea also demonstrate.

Chapter 13, then, is the apocalyptic discourse brought on by a comment about the temple at the center of the city and at the center of Judaism, and chapters 14–16 are the passion narrative proper. Clearly the symbol of Jerusalem and the edifice of the temple dominate the last chapters of Mark's gospel and Jesus' public ministry. Whatever happens from chapter 11 on happens in the shadow of the temple. So let me say a bit about the temple, and then we will double back and think a bit about city as a symbolic location.

The Markan temple was the Second or Herodian temple, not nearly as splendid as Solomon's, but recently "refurbished." As one of Herod's many building projects, the work was begun in 20/19 BC, so was recently completed when Jesus and the disciples arrived. The facade was covered with gold leaf; the sun from the west as the disciples viewed the temple from the Mount of Olives must have made it look quite splendid. During Jesus' lifetime, contemporary attitudes toward the temple varied. For some it was positive, a symbol of God's dwelling with humans and of Israel's election. But there was also a tradition of hostility toward it, especially in apocalyptic thought. For example, in Zechariah 14 the Mount of Olives and Mount Zion are contrasted. (Compare Ezek 40–48 and 1 Enoch 83–90.) There was disagreement among the Jews about whether the temple had to be rebuilt to God's specifications and questions about its contemporary structures and cults. The high priest was named by the Romans, which enraged the Pharisees and, a generation earlier, had been one of the factors that led what became the Qumran community to withdraw into the Judean desert. This is interesting to consider in light of our symbols of desert and city. If the city gets too bad, the desert can look pretty attractive.

My point is that in the Jerusalem temple Mark "inherited" an ambiguous symbol. In contemporary Judaism the temple was the symbol of God's presence with the people of Israel, Israel's cultic life, the forgiveness of sins, and, for Mark, of Israel itself. But only Mark's Jesus, in the temple cleansing episode, says that it is a house of prayer "for all the nations" (11:17, quoting Isa 56:7). Mark is, of course, interested in the Gentile mission (the proclamation of Jesus to people from non-Jewish backgrounds) and is thus uneasy with the racial exclusivity of Judaism. Perhaps for this reason, as well as because of its opposition to his ministry, the Markan Jesus is very hard on the temple and is in controversy with the people he meets there.

We have seen how Jesus takes on official Judaism in 11:27–12:34. Another example occurs in 12:41-44, the story of the widow who gives two copper coins, which is usually read as praise of a good and generous woman. However, read in the context of 12:38-40 which immediately precedes it, I see it as Jesus' attack on a system of religion that would demand of her "all she had to live on." What sort of religious system asks to be supported or even accepts the support of the very people least able to provide it, the most vulnerable in society as certainly a poor widow was in Greco-Roman Jerusalem? No wonder that in 13:2 Jesus condemns the temple.[60]

It seems to me that Mark's gospel asks its readers to replace the temple and its cult with obedience to Jesus, doing what Jesus asks of them. Certainly in the fig tree episode the spiritual focus shifts away from the temple as a *place* of prayer, to prayer itself as the "place" where the faithful meet God. In a book about spiritual geography, it is ironic but true to say that in Jesus' ministry and Mark's theology place isn't *ipso facto* important! Maybe it overstates the case, but I think Mark's whole gospel moves to supplant Jerusalem and the temple. And we see this most clearly when Jesus is actually *in* Jerusalem.

But this, too, is ironic, because it is the Jerusalem section of the gospel that contains the most quotations of and allusions to Hebrew Scripture. In Mark 11–16 there are fifty-seven quotations and one hundred sixty allusions to Hebrew Scripture. Both Jewish Scripture and commonplaces of Jewish thought seem very important in the final week of Jesus' life as the tradition preserved it. Mark gravitates toward eschatological passages and usually quotes the Septuagint, often blending two unrelated verses to make his points. Mark (or the tradition he inherited) uses Hebrew Scripture to depict suffering as part of a divine plan and a precondition for the fulfillment of faith.

That is a very extensive bit of material on Mark's gospel, but I think it is important to the spiritual issues we now want to raise.

The City

Interestingly, our Bible attributes the creation of the first city to Cain. After Cain kills his brother Abel he moves away and, we are told, "he built a city" (Gen 4:17). No wonder that for Mark the city, and Jerusalem itself, is an ambiguous image. It is the religious center of Israel, the locus of religious administration. At its center is the temple, the cultic center of Judaism, the place where God dwells and the place where, on the Day of Atonement, sins are forgiven. But for those of us who try to read the gospel from Jesus' point of view, Jerusalem and the temple are negative images, images of opposition to Jesus, images of religious corruption. For us Jerusalem is the place of the passion, a terrible and a wonderful thing. First of all, then, Jerusalem calls us to hold in tension all the terrible and wonderful paradoxes of our faith.

How closely related good and evil often are! When they move even slightly off center, our greatest spiritual virtues can become our most serious sins. I know that some of the qualities that led me to marry my husband were the very qualities that made it hard to live with him. What we love about people is often also what drives us crazy about them, isn't it? One of the tasks of spiritual maturity is, I think, the task of holding paradoxes in tension, of living in the creativity of that tension no matter how uncomfortable it may be for us to do so. Life is created and flourishes in the tension of opposites. Not all of our tensions can be resolved, which is why it is so important for us to understand the central place of mystery in Christianity.

Mark's symbolic use of Jerusalem and the temple are a call to consider the nature of the church institutional and institutional religion in any of its manifestations: parish, monastery, seminary, family. I find it hard to get the image of "all of Jerusalem" going to the desert and John the Baptist out of my mind. How had the very center of religious life let people down? What was it that was lacking for them, so lacking that they made a very difficult journey to a very unfriendly location to hear a very surprising message? Isn't it interesting that the people of Jerusalem and Judea were so *anxious* to confess their sins and be baptized? At some profound level they seemed to know that they were profoundly broken, wounded, missing the mark. How has the church missed the mark in reaching just these people? I think of the great religious edifices of our faith, the Vatican in Rome, Westminster Abbey in London, Canterbury Cathedral, Saint John the Divine in New York City. How have these great churches failed those who live in their shadows? And "living in the shadows" is, itself, a suggestive turn of phrase, isn't it?

This seems to me a particularly potent question, as well, for those of us who live far from the centers of temporal power and religious authority. What role might we have to play in the exodus of people from today's Jerusalems? Is there a sense in which we are called to be John the Baptist, a prophetic voice, a voice for a more authentic understanding of what it means to be a human being? These are powerful questions. No one else can answer them for you.

Most of the people who read this book will, I assume, be Christians, and therefore in a post-Constantinian world, associated with "religious officialdom." And that means that we must see ourselves *as* Jerusalem and the temple. Most of the people in the world have trouble separating priests, nuns, and persons of serious Christian conviction, from the centers of religious power, and centers of religious power from political power, and political power from corruption. Certainly in America at the moment a certain manifestation of Christianity is hand in glove with political power. I suppose what I am confessing is that I have met the enemy, and I am she. I am Jerusalem and the temple, called to be a city on a hill, a center of spiritual practice and power, but often darkness, not light, partial, even corrupt and corrupting. "Lord have mercy on *me*, a sinner" as I join the throng going from Jerusalem to John in the desert!

What of the city itself, apart from our Markan context? The movement from nomadic to urban existence was a movement, at least symbolically, toward stability. This is why, I think, St. Benedict envisions stability as an important aspect of cenobitic life. Life together—in religious community, in family, in city—is at its best (to use T. S. Eliot's elegant phrase) a still place in a turning world. I am told that nomadic encampments of tents are usually circular, symbolic of movement, but that cities and towns were built as squares, symbolic of stability, like those square Damascene houses we described in chapter 2 after which monasteries were modeled. The square, of course, symbolizes the four directions of the universe and the four elements. In the ancient world, cities were stabilizers because they were often spiritual centers: Heliopolis, city of the sun; Salem, city of peace; Bethel, house of God. Cities were places where temples were built and from which spiritual influence flowed. This is how the "New Jerusalem" functions in John's Revelation. And cities were symbols of empires; out from them flowed the blessings of the king or ruler if he or she were benevolent. "Medieval thinkers saw humanity as a pilgrim between two cities and life as a pilgrimage from the city below to the city above."[61] Perhaps this is why so much medieval and early modern literature is pilgrimage literature. As I suggested earlier, remember the work of Boccacio, Dante, Chaucer, and Bunyan.

Finally, the city is the symbol of community, of our life together. And that, like Mark's Jerusalem, is always an ambiguous business. Religious communities, be they monastic or parish, are usually chosen. We choose a community in part because we love the people already in it and see them as holy, see in those people a vision of what we might be for ourselves and for our Lord. Most people are called into community because it is in community that they can grow toward the person Christ intends them to be. The communal necessity for Christian life was one of the primary insights of that very wise Anglican spiritual theologian, Evelyn Underhill, who wrote: "The Christian . . . cannot fulfill his spiritual obligations in solitude. He forms part of a social and spiritual complex with a new relation to God. . . . Therefore even his most lonely contemplations are not merely a private matter; but always . . . [related] to the purpose and action of God Who incites them, and to the total life of the Church. . . ."[62] Anchorites may be the exception that proves the rule, but, in any case, they are a minority group. Christ calls people into community, because it is there he can best form them and draw them to himself and to each other.

And when we enter those communities, parishes, (families!), we discover the holy people who inhabit them are very, very human indeed. The man you marry squeezes the toothpaste tube from the center instead of rolling it up neatly from the end as sensible people should. Your lovely, interesting children kick their dirty laundry under the bed and refuse to empty the garbage cans. Sister's teeth clack annoyingly when she eats, and she wheezes when she breathes in chapel. Like God's presence and absence in the temple in Jerusalem, in the temple that St. Paul asserts each one of us is, humanity and holiness each have taken up permanent residence. And this is the tension that is life giving, even if it requires the application of spiritual and literal aspirin from time to time!

Community is the place where God dwells, where we can be what Martin Luther King, Jr. called "the beloved community," the place where we rub each other the wrong way and drive each other nuts and can propel each other right into the arms of God. This is the only place we can "fix" our communities and the relationships in them—in the arms of God into which we are all gathered. This is why the way we individually live moment-to-moment, day-to-day, is so important. In 1 Corinthians 6 Paul speaks of our bodies as temples; they are the places where God dwells, from which holiness is to spread, to "infect" those around us. When we, individually, take this vocation seriously, then our lives together become attractive. Like those Judeans and Jerusalemites who were drawn to John the Baptist, so people are drawn to us and to our parishes and religious communities and, through us, to our Lord. Our communities, our life together to use Bonhoeffer's happy phrase, can become like the city on the hill that cannot be hidden. Indeed, that is our vocation as the people of God. *Luceat lux vestra!*

Chapter Six

The Cross/Suffering, Solitariness, and Solidarity[63]

Mark 14–15

> *Almighty God, whose most dear Son went not up to joy but first he suffered pain, and entered not into glory before he was crucified: Mercifully grant that we, walking in the way of the cross, may find it none other than the way of life and peace; through Jesus Christ your Son our Lord, who lives and reigns with you and the Holy Spirit, one God, for ever and ever. Amen.*
>
> —Collect for the Monday in Holy Week,
> *The Book of Common Prayer*[64]

The Cross in Mark's Gospel

Even a cursory reading of Mark's gospel reveals that its author was particularly concerned with suffering and crucifixion. From the beginning of his ministry, Jesus is seen in conflict with those who could do him in. A dark shadow, an ominous atmosphere, pervades the book. The spatial center of Mark's narrative is built around three predictions of Jesus' passion; five of the fifteen full chapters in the gospel deal with the passion week. Robert H. Gundry titles his major and important commentary *Mark: A Commentary on His Apology for the Cross*, and opens that work with the statement that Mark "writes a straightforward apology for the Cross, for the shameful way in which the object of Christian faith and the subject of Christian proclamation died, and hence for Jesus as the Crucified One."[65]

I think Gundry is exactly correct. Mark's immense theological task is to explain the incredible fact of the cross, what Paul so perceptively calls "a stumbling block to Jews and foolishness to Gentiles" (1 Cor 1:23). An "apology" as a literary form is a work that not only seeks to convince the reader of a point of view but also anticipates her or his objections to it and answers them. The Greco-Roman world had not "tamed" the cross by making of it fine jewelry. It was for them an unmitigated horror. Furthermore, Mark is writing for a suffering community, one that has undergone or is undergoing persecution and suffering precisely for its loyalty to its crucified Lord. And so the evangelist wants to connect their suffering with the suffering of Jesus.

One reason Mark's gospel is so helpful to us is that it is a gospel that takes suffering seriously. It doesn't try to sugarcoat it or explain it away with chirpy platitudes. Suffering is part and parcel of the human condition, a given of human life. But, of course, the suffering on which the Gospel rests is chosen suffering. Jesus chose the cross. As we turn to the pastoral reflection on the cross that makes up the substance of this chapter, we do well to make note that there is a difference between chosen suffering and the suffering that is part of life. R. S. Thomas's poem "The Coming" highlights Jesus' choice and serves as a powerful introduction to our topic.

> And God held in his hand
> A small globe. Look, he said.
> The son looked. Far off,
> As though through water, he saw
> A scorched land of fierce
> Colour. The light burned
> There; crusted buildings
> Cast their shadows: a bright
> Serpent, a river
> Uncoiled itself, radiant
> With slime.

> On a bare
> Hill a bare tree saddened
> The sky. Many people
> Held out their thin arms
> To it, as though waiting
> For a vanished April
> To return to its crossed
> Boughs. The son watched
> Them. Let me go there, he said.[66]

A Pastoral Reflection on the Cross

This chapter is different from previous chapters. What I have to say is short, simple, and heartfelt. Suffering in human life is inevitable, but the cross in its solitariness and solidarity is irreversible. We dare not avert our eyes from Jesus on the cross. As he himself said, "And I, when I am lifted up from the earth, will draw all people to myself" (John 12:32). Every life has its Gethsemanes and Calvarys; most have multiple experiences of them. I know something about it. For fourteen months I watched as my husband died of a particularly nasty cancer. It took me years to realize that during those long nights of illness when all I could do to pray was to look at the cross hanging on our bedroom wall, it was God there suffering with us.

I don't know what your personal sufferings have been, but I know you have had them. I don't know what they will be, but I know they will come. And I know that God did not, and will not, abandon you to them. As Jürgen Moltmann so eloquently argued in *The Crucified God*, God suffers with us.[67] In that fact is the irreversibility of the cross. After Calvary no one ever need suffer or die alone. Writing on Psalm 22, American church historian and journalist Martin Marty notes: "The crucified victim was the *only* forsaken one, the true derelict. The rest of us die in company, *his* company. God certified his gift and his act and 'raised him up.' Never again is aloneness to be so stark for others."[68]

The fact of the cross of Jesus Christ in human history is irreversible, both because it is unique in history and because its influence in our history continues. And, as Mark's gospel so clearly dramatizes,

the mystery of the cross is found in its solitariness and solidarity.
Let us reflect a bit on those two points.

Solitariness

There was only one cross of Jesus, one moment in history when
the man from Nazareth was nailed to a Roman cross. On that cross
God gave the Divine Self most fully to human finitude. On that cross
humanity said the definitive "yes" to God. Jesus, whom the Philip-
pian hymn proclaimed equal with God, "emptied himself" to be born
in human likeness, or human appearance (and things aren't always
what they appear!). "He humbled himself and became obedient to
the point of death, even, [it says in quiet horror,] death on a cross"
(Phil 2:7-8). St. John's gospel says Jesus is "the one who descended
from heaven, the Son of Man" (3:13). The Divine-human One came
down and identified himself with the cross, that hideous Hellenistic
symbol of weakness that signified in its world total humiliation and
degradation. No contemporary writer makes this more clear than
Morna Hooker in her 1994 book *Not Ashamed of the Gospel.*

Just as Moses lifted up a brass serpent to heal the sickness of
the Israelites in the wilderness, Jesus was lifted up on the cross of
Calvary to heal our sicknesses. The Divine-human relationship has
always been the story of human rebellion and divine initiative and
self-giving. Genesis 3:8-9 narrates the paradigm of that relationship.
Adam and Eve "heard the sound of the LORD God walking in the
garden at the time of the evening breeze, and the man and his wife
hid themselves from the presence of the LORD God among the trees
of the garden. But the LORD God called . . . and said . . . 'Where
are you?'" God wants to be with us, and, often as not, we hide in
the shrubbery.

This hide-and-seek story reached its culmination when the Son
of Man was "lifted up." "And just as Moses lifted up the serpent in
the wilderness, so must the Son of Man be lifted up" (John 3:14).
He was lifted up on the cross. Abandoned by his friends (Mark
14:43-50, 66-72), condemned by the religious authorities of his own
tradition (Mark 14:53-65; 15:1-15, 29-32), in physical agony and
suffering the pain of knowing his mother and women friends were

there watching his naked body die (Mark 15:33-41), even then Jesus was at the center of Divine will. Even in the midst of what felt like utter abandonment, when he cried out, "My God, my God, why have you forsaken me?" (Mark 15:34), still it was a "yes" to God.

Solidarity

At that moment Jesus was both utterly alone, completely solitary, and in radical solidarity with all human suffering, and with the suffering of God, the pain of God who created the world and humanity in beauty and freedom and who has suffered from our freedom ever since as a parent suffers over a wayward child. The prophet Isaiah had deep insight into God's experience and recorded: "I reared children and brought them up, / but they have rebelled against me. / The ox knows its owner, / and the donkey its master's crib; / but Israel does not know, / my people do not understand" (Isa 1:2b-3).

The prophets of Israel understood God's suffering. In *The Prophets*, Rabbi Abraham Heschel speaks of "Divine pathos" and says, "God is involved in the life of man. A personal relationship binds him to Israel. . . ."[69] If the prophets understood something of the depth of God's suffering, how much more profound was the identification of Jesus with God's agony. Jesus' experience on the cross was one of solitude and solidarity, of bringing together human and divine suffering. That event is irreversible, for on the cross the Divine and human wills were perfectly one.

Deep within each of us is the potential for absolute unity with God, for our cosmic "yes" to the will of God in human life. But we see it most clearly on Calvary's cross where God and humanity came together in a cry of total abandonment and emptiness, and of remarkable, mysterious triumph. There the love of God is proclaimed. God so loved that God gave (John 3:16). The doctrine of the Trinity tells us that God was the Given One. Writing on the Apostles' Creed Alister McGrath concurs, ". . . if it is not God who is dying on the cross, then it is not the love of God that is demonstrated."[70]

As the apostle Paul knew, the cross of Christ would always be a stumbling block. "What kind of God dies?" asked the Greeks of Paul's time, and people in our own day ask it again. Our response can only be: a God who loves us, and who on the cross smashed all our idols of what God ought to look like and be and do. As Morna Hooker notes, "The belief that God is revealed in the shame and weakness of the cross is a profound insight into the nature of God."[71] The message about the cross is foolishness to the perishing, but to us it is the power of God (1 Cor 1:18). This is exactly what Elizabeth Johnson says in her powerful and controversial book, *She Who Is*:

> In the Christian world view the paradigmatic locus of divine involvement in the pain of the world is the cross. In the human integrity of a broken human being, who prized truth and fidelity above his own safety and loved his friends in an ever-widening circle until the godforsaken end, something of the mystery of God is darkly manifest: Christ crucified, the wisdom and power of God. Here if anywhere it can be glimpsed that Wisdom participates in the suffering of the world and overcomes, inconceivably, from within through the power of love.[72]

The cross of Christ is the wisdom and power of God, especially the power of God for the suffering, whoever they are, wherever they are, whatever their suffering is: racism or sexism, economic injustice, military intervention, genocide, physical or mental illness, loneliness, torture, rape . . . whatever the suffering is, the cross stands as witness that God does not abandon us. God suffers with us. In another of her books, Johnson says: "The cross opens a pathway for all the suffering of the world to be taken into the very being of God. God is now so tied into history through his freely given Love on the cross that the pain of the world is admitted into himself. There, the power of divine Love heals, changes, saves it. . . ."[73]

Wounded, Healed and Healing

Moses lifted the brass serpent, and the people lifted their eyes to it and were healed. The Son of Man is lifted up on the cross, and we can lift our eyes to it and be healed. God so loved the world that God provided this healing for individuals and for societies. Jesus provided it in solitude and in solidarity, in giving his body and blood, Semitic metaphors for his very self (*soma*, body), his life (*aima*, blood). Jesus is blessed, broken, and given for us, to make us a people who can be blessed, broken, and given for others. "We are indeed a resurrection people, but also we are a Last Supper people. We are a community which is taken, blessed, broken and given, just as our Saviour was."[74]

Holy Cross Day, September 14, is one of the few commemorations shared by most of the various branches of the Christian family. On Holy Cross Day we "lift high the cross," not to "celebrate" the grue-some death of an innocent man, but in the etymological meaning of "celebrate," to "frequent" it, to become familiar with its effects. To lift high the cross is to see it for what it is: the love of God in the wounds of Jesus. By and large we turn away from wounds, avert our eyes from the person on the street with old incisions or scar tis-sue from burns, from the birth-or-accident deformed. We avoid the mentally ill. It is instinctive, like recoiling from a snake. But it may be the snake that heals.

We don't want to see the wounds. They remind us that we are not perfect. They force us to face our own imperfections, scars, and woundedness. They remind us of all our culture is geared to make us forget. And not looking makes it easier for us to close our eyes to corporate wounds: ghettos, the homeless, the hungry, the mentally ill, the forgotten elderly, the infirm, the AIDS orphan or genocide victim, all the *isms* that distort humanity made in God's image. While it isn't polite to stare, it may be critical to look. Our healing may be found in the snake of our wounds.

Why do we empty the cross of Christ's body? Protestants claim that the focus is resurrection, not crucifixion. But the resurrection was costly. The Easter story in Mark does not proceed from the Triumphal Entry (Palm Sunday) directly to the Empty Tomb. It winds its way through the stations of the cross, by the Via Dolorosa, through an agony of decisions, betrayal, abandonment, mistreat-ment, injustice, torture, crucifixion, and a great cry of dereliction: *Eloi Eloi lema sabachthani* (Mark 15:34). We are healed by Christ's suffering, and we know him by his wounds. In fact, we may know God best through woundedness. It is little wonder that the early

Christians saw in Isaiah 52:13–53:12 the meaning of Jesus' passion. It explains that Jesus was like us, "a man of suffering and acquainted with infirmity" (53:3), that he "was wounded for our transgressions" and "by his bruises we are healed" (53:5).

Saint John the evangelist also understood the importance of the woundedness of Jesus. Because we focus in fascination and identification on St. Thomas, we may forget to notice that in John 20:19-29, Jesus is known by his wounds. On the first Easter Sunday, when he appears in the locked room, Jesus "showed them his hands and his side. *Then* the disciples rejoiced when they saw the Lord" (20:20, italics mine). One week later he says to St. Thomas, "Put your finger here and see my hands. Reach out your hand and put it in my side" (20:27). Jesus offers his wounds not only to be seen, but to be entered into. As Henri Nouwen observed, Jesus made "his own broken body the way to health, to liberation and new life," made "his wounds into a major source of his healing power."[75] John 20:19-29 (compare Luke 24:39) suggests that the wounds (physical, emotional, spiritual) that we so carefully hide are not matters for shame. They are potentially a point of contact with the Risen Christ who can transform them into intimate knowledge of himself.

So this pastoral reflection on the cross becomes a plea for a return of the wounded in our individual lives and in our lives as communities. I think this is consistent with whom Jesus called to accompany him and what the early church was. The healthy don't need a doctor; the sick do (Mark 2:17). In an essay entitled "Salvation as Healing," Donald Gowan writes that "the early church understood its ministry to be the continuation of . . . healing carried out by Jesus." He continues, quoting Harnack's *The Expansion of Christianity*:

> In the world to which the apostles preached their new message, religion had not been intended originally for the sick, but for the sound. The Deity sought the pure and sound to be his worshipers. The sick and sinful, it was held, are the prey of the powers of darkness; let them see to the recovery of health by some means or other, health for the soul and body—for until then they are not pleasing to the gods.[76]

The apostle Paul understood Christianity to have a very different view, indeed. "For while we were still weak . . . Christ died for the ungodly. . . . But God proves his love for us in that while we still were sinners Christ died for us" (Rom 5:6, 8). Christ died for us when we were weak, sick, and sinful. "Christianity never lost hold of its innate principle; it was, and it remained, a religion for the sick."[77]

When it came out, Henri Nouwen's book *The Wounded Healer* had a profound effect on me. Nouwen wrote: "the wound, which causes us to suffer now, will be revealed to us later as the place where God intimated his new creation."[78] Our wounds are potentially the source of our healing because they draw us to Christ the wounded God and to each other. For woundedness is our common condition; we humans share it with one another and with God. The church should be a community that, because it can look on the broken body of Jesus, is a place where the wounded are seen and welcomed, where wounds are transformed and become a witness to faith and an invitation to faithfulness.

That "Christ died for us" does not mean we escape woundedness, suffering, and death. I think that Mark's gospel is not only an apology for the scandal of the cross but an extended meditation on the profound connection between discipleship and the suffering and death of Jesus. As Mark 8:34-35 intimates, if we wish to share Christ's triumph, we must be willing to share his shame and death. No cross, no crown. And if we are to bring Christ to the world, which I believe is part of our calling as the church, then we will occasionally find ourselves hanging there on the cross before it, naked and bleeding. It's not a pretty sight, but it is a healing one, and a profound point of identification with our Lord.

Our own suffering can bring us very close to Jesus. But the suffering of those we know, those we serve, those with whom we live, also gifts us with God's presence. As Johnson writes, "Suffering people are the privileged place where the God of compassion is to be found."[79] Because Jesus was lifted up on the cross, all those who suffer are ultimately lifted up by the living, loving God. Because of love for us, God "determined to experience firsthand what it is like to be frail, mortal and human, to suffer and to die. . . . [I]n the person of His son Jesus Christ, God took it upon himself to follow this way. God became the 'man of suffering' so that we can enter into the mystery of death and resurrection."[80] Because Jesus is lifted up in suffering, God lifts up the suffering. The cross is the point of God's radical identification with suffering. It is where earth and heaven meet and, as such, the most important "place" in the spiritual landscape we have been exploring.

I cannot explain suffering. This chapter does not answer the problem of theodicy. I am not sure that human suffering is even potentially redemptive. But I do know it is not faced alone. And, as Elizabeth Johnson writes, "Knowing that we are not abandoned makes all the difference."[81] At the cross we find the essence of the Good News, that "we are more than conquerors through him who loved us. . . . neither death, nor life, nor angels, nor rulers, nor things present, nor things to come, nor powers, nor height, nor depth, nor anything else in all creation, will be able to separate us from the love of God in Christ Jesus our Lord" (Rom 8:37-39).

Chapter Seven

The Garden/Resurrection . . . Perhaps

Mark 14:32-42; 16:1-8

 *Heavenly Father, we approach your Son's resurrection with joy and with fear. It is, as birth always is, filled with delight and danger. Bring resurrection to our lives in spite of us. May we allow you to roll the stones away from all that entombs us, to set us free to liberate those around us. Help us to surrender to you that we may be victorious through him who loved us and gave himself for us. Amen.*

Introduction

As a general rule, gospels end on a note of triumph. In the popular imagination, at least, the gospels end as the faithful women trudge in darkness to the garden where, in Cecil B. DeMille fashion, brilliant light and a blonde angel emerge from the tomb to say that everything is going to be all right. Similarly, retreats or books like this one end with a sort of pep talk that, in outline, goes like this: we have spent this time with Jesus, and he has strengthened us for service (Rah-rah). So let's go out and do it, do it, do it (Rah-rah-rah). In short, we get a modern spin on *en hoc signu vincus.*

But Mark's gospel, and thus I fear this little book, ends on rather a more somber and subdued note. The last words of Mark's gospel are "for they were afraid," *ephobounto gar.* A stone rolled back and an angelic messenger, yes. But no risen Jesus, no lakeside picnic, no traveler on the road who stays for tea, no mysterious gardener who knows our name, *nada, nada, nada.* Only the message that Jesus is resurrected, the command to tell Peter and the others to go back to Galilee—the same old home place—and three terrified women who may or may not tell anybody anything.

Having persevered this far with me in the journey, you probably have intuited I am something of an Eeyore. But the fact is, I think 16:8 is exactly the right ending for Mark's gospel, written as it was for Christians under persecution who were themselves faced with martyrdom, focusing as it does on the cross. And I think it is the right ending for us. This is where we live: after the resurrection but before the Return, entrusted with a message that is wonderful, but the import of which we don't quite understand. Mark 16:6-8 is the space most of us inhabit if we are honest with ourselves.

Mark's gospel ends in two gardens and neither of them is exactly the restoration of Eden: the Garden of Gethsemane, the garden of agony and decision; and the Garden of Resurrection, the garden of new life, but of mysterious, uncertain new life. (Of course it is from John's gospel that we take the garden image; Mark doesn't make that explicit.) As recent history in the United States demonstrates, what is mysterious, uncertain, and unknown is often feared. Even if what is promised is wonderful, if it is mysterious, it is approached tentatively and with uncertainty.

I prefer Holy Saturday to Easter morning. As it happens in my Eeyore-ian theology, Holy Saturday is the high feast day of my church year. I think about it a lot. I hope you will indulge me as I include two poems about Holy Saturday.[82] They suggest the dual themes of this last chapter, uncertainty and expectation, or, put another way, unknowing and hope. We don't exactly know what comes next, but we trust it to be resurrective.

The Third Day

Dead grass erupted
through dirty snow

in gray, scrofulous patches
as, day before yesterday,
fog the color of dirty dishwater
fell like a dark curtain
in an isolation ward,
imprisoning the world
in a nightmare
of dissolution and ooze.

Yesterday, heavy, wet snow
covered those horrors
in yards of misshapen cotton wool.
Although early morning,
other creatures had precedence.
Deer, birds, a rabbit,
something ominously feline
left tracks before the sun
rose in blinding revelation
of life's connectedness.

On this, the third day,
the merest of appearances:
the tips of daffodils
roll back stones,
take a tentative peek
from the frozen grave.
In astonished stillness,
everything holds its breath
waiting to see
what will happen next.

Holy Saturday

After the night of tears,
the noon of darkness,
a whole day's space,
the seventh day,
the day God rested

from making,
from being unmade.

Christ has died.
Life is hidden
in God's obscurity.
Adam lays bounded
with fruitless Eve.
Nobody can be sure
what will happen next.

I love this day
of silent waiting
when fasting is over,
feasting not begun,
when pain is past
but flesh not quickened.
This is where we live,

this human space,
waiting before the cave
in the tarnished garden
where it all began
and ended
to begin anew,
we hope, forever.

Waiting to see what will happen next, waiting, we hope, to begin anew. This is where we are at the end of Mark's gospel, an ending and a beginning to which we now turn.

Mark 16:1-8

The most ancient manuscripts of Mark show no knowledge of 16:9-20, which reflect two alternative endings. Scholarly consensus is that Mark ends with 16:8, and that the other verses were added later by other hands. Some think Mark never finished the gospel, others that his "real" conclusion was lost or destroyed or even deliberately suppressed. I don't think this is the place to rehearse the arguments for and against 16:1-8 as the ending. In my view, attestation, style, content, and theology all declare that what comes after 16:8 is non-Markan, an addition by a later hand to bring the ending of Mark into line with the other gospels, a "cheering up" of Mark's uncertain ending.

My own sense is that 16:1-8 is exactly the right ending for Mark's gospel. In an odd way it points again to the cross and its meaning. Mark's audience knew the facts of the gospel as we do. They knew Jesus had been raised (passive voice again, Someone Else raised him) from the dead. Jesus' resurrection is presupposed, but Mark thinks it must be understood in terms of the cross. Stylistically, the brevity of the ending parallels the brevity of the opening, "both alike being outside the main purpose of the evangelist."[83] As R. H. Lightfoot observed years ago, the crucified Messiah as the fulfillment of God's promise is the chief theme of Mark's gospel.[84]

Why omit resurrection appearances, which certainly Mark knew from the oral tradition of the church? Perhaps he did so for theological consistency. Throughout the gospel Mark demonstrates that faith is generated by the word of Jesus and not by miracle. Jesus' message was repeatedly misunderstood, even as his miracles were sought. Those who were with Jesus in Roman Palestine and those who come to believe through his words are, in fact, equals. Mark (like John, in fact, see John 20:29), places no special value on "being there." What counts is responding to the message.

Mark's resurrection account begins in 15:42-47 and continues in chapter 16 with a beautiful account of the devotion of the women and a dark picture of the male disciples who, throughout the gospel, have misunderstood Jesus and are now absent. Up to this point the women have been paradigmatic disciples, the men the negative examples. But now the women, too, are shown in darkness. They, too, misunderstand and fear. Mark's point: no disciple is perfect. All discipleship is partial and flawed. All disciples are wounded.

What of the women's fearful silence? Perhaps it is another example of Mark's realism. The women are afraid because they have come to a cemetery to anoint a corpse. Or perhaps it is the fear of women without a male to protect them. Or perhaps they are afraid, as they might well be, of the Roman or Jewish authorities. "Fear" is the usual response to the unexpected throughout Mark's gospel. Suppose the young man in white was thought by them to *be* Jesus, provoking an "it might be—it can't be" response. Or perhaps, as I suspect, the picture is of human inadequacy and lack of understanding in the face of supreme and divine action. Who understands when God's power is manifested among us?

A. T. Lincoln has written a helpful essay titled "The Promise and the Failure: Mark 16:7-8."[85] In it he suggests that the juxtaposition of verses 7 and 8 provide a paradigm of Christian existence according to Mark: a word of promise and the failure of human disciples, but the word of promise predominates for the future. The ending of Mark is an encouragement to persevere despite failure. If disciples and witnesses fail (as they did, and do, and will), the cause is not necessarily lost. I find this an immensely helpful and practical suggestion. It makes Mark 16:8 a beginning rather than an ending. It leaves the propagation of the gospel of resurrection precisely with us. Like the women at the tomb, we have heard the witness of resurrection. Will we proclaim it? Will we be resurrected persons? Or will we live in fear of the mysteriousness of resurrection and what it calls us to do?

Three things emerge from the ending of Mark's gospel. First, 16:8 recalls that dread or fear or uncertainty as well as love and faith and assurance are essential notes in Christianity. The Jesus who is "good above all other / gentle child of gentle mother"[86] and the Jesus of the agony of the Garden of Gethsemane and the hill of Calvary coexist in each of us. Uncertainty is not unbelief, and darkness of understanding is not damnation. Second, Mark's purpose is to get the reader/hearer of the gospel to confess that Jesus, Messiah and Son of God, is the One God appointed to die on the cross. That is why the confession that Jesus is Son of God comes only at his death by crucifixion and only on the lips of a Gentile centurion (15:39). The resurrection is God's way of affirming Jesus. But crucifixion is God's way in the world. Jesus' resurrection is his vindication and the one that his disciples await as well. But a happily-ever-after ending isn't consistent with Mark's theology. So, finally, the renewed promise of Christ to all his disciples in verse 7 is a word of promise in spite of their denial. As Paul reminds the Corinthians, in Christ "every one of God's promises is a 'Yes'" (2 Cor 1:20). Human fear and failure is always trumped by Divine forgiveness and mercy. And for this disciple of Jesus who loves him and wants to do his will but is fearful, failing, flawed, and foolish, that is very, very good news.

The Image of the Garden

Let us close by doubling back to the image of the garden, the primordial symbol of the Earthly Paradise, and prefiguration of the Heavenly Paradise. The garden is the locus of life at its most fruitful and most beautiful. Ancient Semitic peoples were enamored of gardens perhaps because of the contrast they made with the aridity of their surroundings. The juxtaposition of desert and garden is an invitation, as the garden invites the desert to return to its original state and nature. Both Christianity and Islam (see Koran 18:55) image the heavenly paradise as a garden, an oasis. The image is of fruitfulness at the center, the water of life at the heart of life together. John uses just this image in chapter 22 of the book of the Revelation to John.

The garden is a primary biblical symbol as well. I learned a good deal about it from a ninety-year-old Daughter of Wisdom in London called Sister Phillip who sent me notes of a talk she gave on gardens. The account of salvation history itself begins in a garden. At the outset God plants a garden which he gives into human keeping. Why a garden? Perhaps because we are drawn most easily to God by beauty. Humanity's first wedding was a garden wedding. God met his friends in that garden until they overstepped the borders of God's hospitality and were sent out of the garden. And the rest of the biblical narrative is the story of God calling people back to the garden of Divine intention for them or of people struggling their way back. God wants to walk with us in the cool of the evening.

Salvation history begins in a garden and makes its slow, painful way to the New Jerusalem which, in Revelation 21–22, is an eternally fruitful garden city, an oasis. And the route from the one to the other passes directly through the Garden of Gethsemane and the Garden of Resurrection. Without the suffering discernment and decision of Gethsemane there can be no resurrection. And without the resurrection there can be no New Jerusalem. Jesus suffered in a garden in order to be laid to rest in a garden. God raised him up in a garden that we might dwell eternally in a garden. I am never very surprised that so many people are such avid gardeners. It is a tiny way that we cooperate with God's intentions for creation. On the level of archetype, we gardeners are working our way back to Eden or forward to the oasis of the New Jerusalem. It is in our genes to do this, I think. We are "hot-wired" for it.

Eden. Gethsemane. Resurrection. New Jerusalem. In the midst of the positive images of garden in the Bible stands the darkness of Gethsemane. In the church in which I grew up, my favorite stained glass window was in the back wall of the balcony, a window of Jesus in the Garden. It was a dark window. Up under the roof, it got little light, so the sky in the picture was black-navy and the space around Jesus was dark. In the window Jesus, wearing a white robe, the only light color in the window, is kneeling, leaning against a huge, gray boulder, and looking imploringly upward. I loved that window. I suppose in some oblique way, even as a small child, I knew that it depicted what would be my own, fundamental spiritual disposition—reaching out in darkness to God.

It is a bit of a stretch, but I suggest that in the two great gardens at the close of Mark's gospel, Gethsemane and Resurrection, there is a stone at the center. In my mind's eye there is always that great stone on which Jesus leaned to pray in the Gethsemane stained glass window. Imagine how I felt when I discovered that at the traditional site of Gethsemane, the Church of all Nations in Jerusalem at the foot of the Mount of Olives, great stones protrude through the floor of the nave.

In the accounts of the Garden of Resurrection in the gospels there is the great stone over the mouth of Jesus' tomb. Who will move it? The women know that they are unable to remove what separates them from the Lord. This is a great metaphor for the spiritual life. We cannot, in our own strength, remove what separates us from God and the life God wants us to have in fullness. We cannot bring life from death. But God can and does. The technical word for this is "grace."

Psalm 118:22-23 provides an interesting gloss on the stone. "The stone that the builders rejected / has become the chief cornerstone. / This is the LORD's doing; / it is marvelous in our eyes." The important bit for the point I am making is "This is the LORD's doing." The work is God's. Our task is to surrender to it. Perhaps my poem "The Stone" captures better what I am trying to say:

> The Myrrh bearers came
> (with what fear and trembling?)
> trudging alone in darkness
> worrying about
> the stone.
>
> Everybody worries about
> the stone,
> that great impediment
> between us
> and what we seek,
>
> that great burden
> we carry
> like Sisyphus
> laboring
> up and down the hill.
>
> The sun rose.
> The women looked up.
> The stone,
> which was very large,
> had been removed.
>
> No wonder they ran
> to tell Cephas.
> Somebody should tell Sisyphus:
> "Put it down, man,
> and dance on it."[87]

Almost everything about the resurrection of Jesus is beyond me. I don't understand it. Like the women at the end of Mark's gospel, I am amazed and more than a little afraid. But the bit of the resurrection that I do understand is the removal of the stone. The women come as darkness gives way to daylight to discover that the stone has been moved for them. What Christianity teaches us is that in spite of ourselves, our fears, our failures, our insufficiencies, our woundedness, the stone has been moved for us. What stone remains for you? Will you allow God to move it? You probably can't move it yourself. The crucial question is like the one John's Jesus put to the paralytic: "Do you want it to be moved?"

Here we are, the recipients of a message from a heavenly messenger. He tells us not to be afraid. He tells us that the risen Jesus *goes before us*—is not in our known past, but in the uncertainty and insecurity of our unknown future. There we will see him as he promised. And so we, too, leave the Garden of Resurrection. To do what?

Notes

[1] C. S. Lewis, *Letters to Malcolm, Chiefly on Prayer* (London: Collins/ Fontana, 1966), 76.

[2] Thomas Merton, *Entering the Silence: The Journals of Thomas Merton, Volume 2: 1941–1952*, ed. Jonathan Montaldo (San Francisco: HarperSanFrancisco, 1996), 216.

[3] Charles de Foucauld, *Charles de Foucauld: Writings*, ed. Robert Ellsberg, Modern Spiritual Masters Series (Maryknoll: Orbis Press, 1999), 78.

[4] Bonnie Thurston, *Preaching Mark* (Minneapolis: Fortress Press, 2002).

[5] See John R. Donahue, SJ, "Windows and Mirrors: The Setting of Mark's Gospel," *CBQ* 57, no. 1 (1995): 1–26; and an alternative view, Joel Marcus, "The Jewish War and the Sitz im Leben of Mark," *JBL* 3 (1992): 441–62.

[6] See Jean Chevalier and Alain Gheerbrant, eds., *The Penguin Dictionary of Symbols* (London: Penguin Books, 1996), 167–72.

[7] Bede Griffiths, *Bede Griffiths: Essential Writings*, ed. Thomas Matus, Modern Spiritual Masters Series (Maryknoll: Orbis Press, 2004), 32.

[8] Ibid.

[9] Evelyn Underhill, *The Spiritual Life* (Harrisburg, PA: Morehouse Publishing, 1955), 32.

[10] Griffiths, *Bede Griffiths*, 80.

[11] R. S. Thomas, *The Poems of R. S. Thomas* (Fayetteville, AR: University of Arkansas Press, 1985), 82. © Kunjana Thomas 2001. Used with permission.

[12] An earlier draft of this chapter was given in February 2002 as a Price Lecture at Trinity Church, Copley Square, Boston.

[13] Andrew Louth, *The Wilderness of God* (Nashville: Abingdon Press, 1991), 46.

[14] Ibid.

[15] S. G. F. Brandon, "The Date of the Markan Gospel," *NTS* 7 (1960/61): 128.

[16] Mary Ann Tolbert, "Asceticism and Mark's Gospel," in *Asceticism and the New Testament*, eds. L. E. Vaage and V. L. Wimbush, 30–48 (London: Routledge, 1999), 30.

[17] "*Eremos*" in Gerhard Kittel, *Theological Dictionary of the New Testament* (Grand Rapids: Eerdmans, 1964) II: 657.

[18] R. S. Thomas, *The Poems of R. S. Thomas*, 129. © Kunjana Thomas 2001. Used with permission.

[19] Howard C. Kee, "The Function of Scriptural Quotations and Allusions in Mark 11–16," in *Jesus und Paulus*, eds. E. E. Ellis and E. Grasser (Gottingen: Vandenhoeck and Ruprecht, 1975), 165–88.

[20] For more on this idea see John Paul Heil, "Jesus with the Wild Animals in Mark 1:13," *CBQ* 68 (2006): 63–78.

[21] Kittel, *Theological Dictionary*, II: 658.

[22] Peter France, *Hermits: The Insights of Solitude* (New York: St. Martin's Press, 1996), 26, 29.

[23] Blaise Pascal, *Pensees: Thoughts on Religion and Other Subjects*, trans. William F. Trotter, ed. H. S. Thayer (NY: Washington Square Press, 1965), 43.

[24] Louth, *Wilderness of God*, 140.

[25] Kittel, *Theological Dictionary*, II: 658.

[26] Tolbert, "Asceticism and Mark's Gospel," 36.

[27] Elizabeth Struthers Malbon, "Disciples, Crowds, Whoever: Markan Characters and Readers," *NovT* 28 (1986a): 112.

[28] Richard Rohrbaugh, "The Social Location of the Markan Audience," *Interpretation* 74, no. 4 (1993): 388–89.

[29] Tolbert, "Asceticism and Mark's Gospel," 40.

[30] Ibid., 44.

[31] Eduard Schweizer, "The Portrayal of the Life of Faith in the Gospel of Mark," *Interpretation* 74, no. 4 (1978): 397.

[32] Malbon, "Disciples, Crowds, Whoever," 113.

[33] "O, Master, Let Me Walk with Thee," words by Washington Gladden, 1879, stanza 4.

[34] Quoted in John Moses, ed., *The Desert: An Anthology for Lent* (Harrisburg, PA: Morehouse, 1997), 26.

[35] Louth, *Wilderness of God*, 40–41.

[36] Moses, *The Desert*, 12.

[37] Antoine de Saint-Exupéry, *The Little Prince* (New York: Harcourt, Brace, and World, 1943) 75.

[38] Chevalier and Gheerbrant, *Penguin Dictionary of Symbols*, 529–31.

[39] See Vernon S. MacCasland, "'Abba' Father," *JBL* 72 (1953): 79–91.

[40] de Foucauld, *Charles de Foucauld*, 68.

[41] Ibid., 90.

[42] Chevalier and Gheerbrant, *Penguin Dictionary of Symbols*, 836–38.

[43] Bonnie Thurston, "Faith and Fear in the Gospel of Mark," *Bible Today* 23, no. 5 (1985): 305–10.

[44] Chevalier and Gheerbrant, *Penguin Dictionary of Symbols*, 1060.

[45] Ibid., 1060–61.

[46] See Thomas Merton, "The Root of War is Fear," chap. 16 in *New Seeds of Contemplation* (New York: New Directions, 1961).

[47] Ernst Best, *Disciples and Discipleship* (Edinburgh: T and T Clark, 1986), 13.

[48] Chevalier and Gheerbrant, *Penguin Dictionary of Symbols*, 557.

[49] Quoted in Andrew Rasanen, "Pilgrimage: Paths to the Center," *Religion and Society* supplement to *Harvard University Gazette* March 27, 1987, 5.

[50] Phil Cousineau, *The Art of Pilgrimage* (Berkeley, CA: Conari Press, 1998), xx.

[51] Ibid., 88.

[52] Ibid., 82.

[53] Thomas Merton, *Thoughts in Solitude* (New York: Farrar, Straus and Giroux, 1956), 56.

[54] Two helpful and accessible articles on the transfiguration are Herbert W. Basser, "The Jewish Roots of Transfiguration," *Bible Review* 14, no. 3 (1998): 30–35, and Jerome Murphy-O'Connor, OP, "What Really Happened at the Transfiguration?" *Bible Review* 3, no. 3 (1987): 8–21.

[55] C. S. Mann, *Mark*, Anchor Bible (Garden City, NY: Doubleday, 1986), 354–68.

[56] Merton, *Thoughts in Solitude*, 56.

[57] Catherine Aslanoff, ed. *The Incarnate God: The Feasts of Jesus Christ and the Virgin Mary*, vol. 2, trans. Paul Meyendorff (New York: St. Vladimir's Seminary Press, 1995), 37.

[58] A particularly helpful article and one that has influenced my thinking is John Paul Heil's "The Narrative Strategy and Pragmatics of the Temple Theme in Mark," *CBQ* 59, no. 1 (1997): 76–100.

[59] A wonderful study on these troubling verses is Sharyn Dowd's *Prayer, Power, and the Problem of Suffering*, SBLDS 105 (Atlanta: Scholars Press, 1988).

[60] For more on this reading see Elizabeth Struthers Malbon, "The Poor Widow in Mark and His Poor Rich Readers," *CBQ* 53 (1991):589–604 and

A. G. Wright, "The Widow's Mite: Praise or Lament?—A Matter of Context," *CBQ* 44 (1982):256–65.

[61] Chevalier and Gheerbrant, *Penguin Dictionary of Symbols*, 204. See also Barbara Tuchman, *A Distant Mirror* (NY: Knopf, 1978).

[62] Emilie Griffin, ed. *Evelyn Underhill: Essential Writings*, Modern Spiritual Masters Series (Maryknoll, NY: Orbis Books, 2003), 109.

[63] Part of his material appeared first as a sermon I gave when installed as the William F. Orr Chair in New Testament at Pittsburgh Theological Seminary, Pittsburgh, PA. It was subsequently printed in expanded form in the seminary's magazine, *Panorama* 34, no. 4 (1999). Another version was given as a talk to an ecumenical Lenten gathering in Winchester, England.

[64] Collect for the Monday in Holy Week, *The Book of Common Prayer* (According to use of The Episcopal Church) (New York: Oxford University Press, 1979), 220.

[65] Robert H. Gundry, *Mark: A Commentary on His Apology for the Cross* (Grand Rapids: Eerdmans, 1993), 1.

[66] R. S. Thomas, *The Poems of R. S. Thomas*, 82–83. © Kunjana Thomas 2001. Used with permission.

[67] Jürgen Moltmann, *The Crucified God* (New York: Harper and Row, 1974).

[68] Martin Marty, *A Cry of Absence* (San Francisco: Harper and Row, 1983), 139.

[69] Abraham J. Heschel, *The Prophets* (New York: Harper and Row, 1969), 24.

[70] Alister McGrath, *"I Believe": Exploring the Apostles' Creed* (Downers Grove, IL: InterVarsity Press, 1997), 65.

[71] Morna Hooker, *Not Ashamed of the Gospel* (Grand Rapids: Eerdmans, 1994), 141.

[72] Elizabeth Johnson, *She Who Is* (New York: Crossroad, 1992), 263.

[73] Elizabeth Johnson, *Consider Jesus* (New York: Crossroad, 1992), 121.

[74] Lavinia Byrne, *Women at the Altar* (Collegeville, MN: Liturgical Press, 1994), 105.

[75] Henri Nouwen, *The Wounded Healer* (New York: Doubleday Image, 1979), 82, 83.

[76] Donald Gowan, "Salvation as Healing," *Ex Auditu* 5 (1989): 13.

[77] Harnack quoted in Gowan, "Salvation as Healing," 13.

[78] Nouwen, *The Wounded Healer*, 96.

[79] Johnson, *Consider Jesus*, 126.

[80] McGrath, "*I Believe*," 66.

[81] Johnson, *Consider Jesus*, 267.

[82] I have written both poems. "Holy Saturday" appears in *Hints and Glimpses* (Abergavenny: Three Peaks Press, 2004), 47.

[83] E. Gould, *The Gospel According to St. Mark*, ICC (New York: Charles Scribner's Sons, 1913), 304.

[84] R. H. Lightfoot, *The Gospel Message of St. Mark* (Oxford: Oxford University Press, 1962), 31.

[85] A. T. Lincoln, "The Promise and the Failure: Mark 16:7, 8," *JBL* 108 (1989): 283–300.

[86] *The Hymnal of the Protestant Episcopal Church* (New York: Church Pension Fund, 1940) #322.

[87] Thurston, *Hints and Glimpses*, 49.